Stephen Wehrmann, D.V.M.
Revised by Sharon L. Vanderlip, D.V.M.

Lhasa Apsos

Everything About Purchase, Care,
Nutrition, Behavior, and Training

Filled with Full-color
Photographs

Illustrations by
Michele Earle-Bridges

BARRON'S

2 CONTENTS

Somewhere in a mystical, faraway land of intense cold, sweltering heat, rugged mountains, and steep valleys lies the birthplace of the Lhasa Apso breed. For hundreds—maybe thousands— of years the bright and bold Lhasa guarded village homes in its native Tibet.

Origin of the Breed

Named after the sacred city of Lhasa (the capital city of Tibet), this charming little canine, admired for its courage and protectiveness, was so highly prized that it could not leave the country unless it was offered as a gift from the Dalai Lama.

In many ways, time has stood still for the Lhasa Apso, which remained geographically isolated and changed little over the centuries. Known as Abso Seng Kye, or the "Bark Lion Sentinel Dog," Lhasas were kept indoors as special guardians because of their intelligence, keen sense of hearing, ability to quickly differentiate friend from foe, and loud warning barks.

For centuries the Lhasa Apso was considered a rare and precious treasure in its native Tibet. Today this extraordinary canine has captured the hearts and imaginations of dog lovers worldwide.

"Apso" may be derived from the Tibetan word "rapso," meaning "goatlike," because of the breed's long, thick coat. In some countries the Lhasa Apso is referred to as the Tibetan Apso. Although there is little recorded history for this ancient breed, we do know that Lhasas are rooted firmly in Tibetan folklore and culture. For hundreds of years it was considered a great honor to receive a Lhasa Apso from the Dalai Lama, an honor sometimes bestowed on visiting dignitaries from other countries. A Lhasa was believed to bring its owner good luck. Some folklore suggests that Lhasas were involved in religious ceremonies in Tibet and considered sacred because the souls of deceased Dalai Lamas were thought to enter the bodies of the Lhasa Apsos.

The first Lhasa Apsos imported to the United States arrived in 1933. They were a gift from the thirteenth Dalai Lama to naturalist C. Suydam Cutting, from Hamilton Farms in New Jersey. Cutting had traveled to Tibet and formed a friendship with the Tibetan leader.

American Kennel Club Group Classifications

Group	Classification
Group I	Sporting Dogs
Group II	Hounds
Group III	Working Dogs
Group IV	Terriers
Group V	Toys
Group VI	Non-Sporting Dogs
Group VII	Herding Dogs
Miscellaneous Class	

In 1935, the Lhasa Apso was admitted to American Kennel Club (AKC) registration and classified in the Terrier Group. Recognizing that the classification was not an accurate one for the breed, the AKC reassigned the Lhasa Apso to the Non-Sporting Group in 1939, where it has remained ever since.

The Lhasa Apso Standard

A Lhasa's personality is as important as its endearing appearance. That is why Lhasa character is included and described in the official standard. Lhasas should be outgoing and happy, confident and bold, but cautious around strangers.

Lhasas come in various colors including honey, sand, slate, or black brindle. The coat is heavy, dense, and straight and should not be silky or woolly.

Size ranges from 10 to 11 inches (25.4 to 28 cm) at the shoulders, females usually being smaller than males. Weight is from 13 to 15 pounds (6 to 7 kg) and should not exceed 18 pounds (8 kg).

A nicely balanced Lhasa is longer that it is tall, with well-developed loins and shoulders. The muzzle is of medium length, with the length from the nose to eye being roughly about one-third of the total length from the nose to the

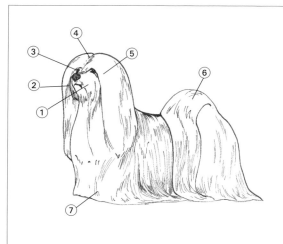

Illustrated Standard

1 Fairly narrow head covered with heavy furnishings, especially whiskers and beard
2 Level or slightly undershot bite
3 Medium-sized eyes
4 Narrow skull, not quite flat
5 Pendant, heavily feathered ears
6 Tail carried over back in a screw
7 Round feet

❏ **Color:** any
❏ **DQ:** none

DQ = Disqualification

Group VI: Non-Sporting Dogs

Bichon Frise
Boston Terrier
Bulldog
Chinese Shar-Pei
Chow Chow
Dalmatian
Finnish Spitz
French Bulldog
Keeshond
Lhasa Apso
Poodle
Schipperke
Tibetan Spaniel
Tibetan Terrier

back of the skull. The eyes are dark brown, medium-sized, and expressive. The ears are pendant and covered thickly with hair, as are all four legs. The tail is carried over the back in a corkscrew and there may be a kink at the end.

The Lhasa Apso's Place in the Dog World

The Lhasa Apso is a member of the Non-Sporting Group (AKC classification Group VI), which consists of several of the more unusual or exotic breeds of dogs, including two other breeds that share their native home with the Lhasa: the Tibetan Terrier and the Tibetan Spaniel.

Parts of a Lhasa Apso.

1. *muzzle*
2. *stop*
3. *skull*
4. *cheek*
5. *neckline*
6. *ears*
7. *shoulder*
8. *withers*
9. *rib cage*
10. *tail*
11. *loin*
12. *stifle*
13. *hindquarters*
14. *hock*
15. *rear pastern*
16. *front pastern*
17. *forequarters*
18. *brisket*
19. *chest*

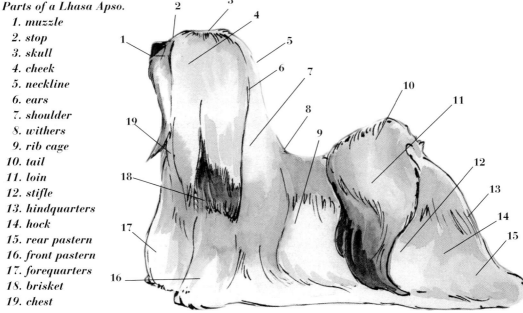

CONSIDERATIONS BEFORE YOU BUY

You meet a Lhasa Apso for the first time and suddenly find yourself enchanted by this magical, mysterious, ancient breed. Its charm and confidence, endearing appearance, portable size, and bright countenance have a luring appeal that sets it apart from all other canine breeds.

Is a Lhasa Apso the Right Dog for You?

You admire the little dog's bold, feisty behavior and strong temperament. Naturally you wonder if a Lhasa Apso just might be the perfect dog for you. Because Lhasa Apsos can live 10 to 15 years or more, you want to be sure that your lifestyles and personalities are compatible.

There is a lot to learn about Lhasas and their care and some distinct advantages to owning a small dog. If you want an indoor dog, or just don't have the space for a larger breed dog, a Lhasa Apso may be the ideal candidate for you. Just remember that all dogs require daily exercise, and a Lhasa is no exception. A daily walk on a

Your Lhasa Apso has an impressive pedigree and is the product of countless generations of selective breeding. This Lhasa pup, standing on the steps of remote Tibet, a close cousin to your precious pet.

leash, or a romp in the yard, will help keep your companion physically fit and in good health.

Lhasas may be small, but they have a lot of hair! Their beautiful, heavy coats evolved over the centuries to protect them from the severe weather conditions encountered in Tibet. You will have to set aside time for regular grooming sessions (see HOW-TO: Grooming Your Lhasa Apso) to keep your Lhasa's skin and coat healthy. A well-groomed Lhasa is nothing less than stunning and attracts admirers like a magnet. Just wait until you go for a walk with your pet. You'll see!

Pesonality

Every Lhasa has its own unique personality, but there are distinct behavioral and inherited (genetic) traits distinctive of the breed—traits that are deeply engrained in these courageous, lively little dogs. The same characteristics that have made the Lhasa Apso a valuable asset as a guardian of the imperial families of Tibet and China for hundreds of years are the same ones

Lhasa Apso Quiz

Here's a little quiz to help you determine if a Lhasa Apso is the right dog for you.

1 Do you enjoy the company of a dog that is cute, cuddly, and portable?

2 Are you looking for a dog that is courageous, loyal, and protective?

3 Can you provide enough time and love for a dog that craves attention and wants to be part of every family activity?

4 Are you able to find the time to exercise your dog every day?

5 Can you set aside time on a regular basis to groom your pet?

6 Do you have the patience for a dog that is not just alert and appealing, but assertive, intelligent, and sometimes mischievous?

If you have answered "yes" to these questions, then you just might be ready to join the ranks of hundreds of people who have owned and loved Lhasa Apsos!

that make the Lhasa Apso a treasured watchdog for modern-day families. They include an alert and protective nature, well-developed senses of hearing and smell, and a ready voice. Lhasas can easily distinguish friend from stranger. They are wary of strangers and are quick to bark a warning alarm when they encounter an intruder or feel threatened.

Some Lhasas have been accused of being dominant, overbearing, or even aggressive, but such animals are the exception. It is true that Lhasas can sometimes be strong-willed, and even stubborn, but this spirited behavior is a survival mechanism that is part of the Lhasa Apso heritage. Without such boldness, this small canine breed could not have survived in its harsh and threatening environment throughout the centuries.

In reality, a well-socialized Lhasa Apso is even-tempered, good-natured, and well-mannered. Because they are so intelligent, they are easy to train and eager to please. Lhasas thrive on human companionship and attention and are quick to return affection.

The Commitment

Whether to bring a new dog into your life, and when to do it, are major decisions that require serious consideration before you take action. Dog ownership, or guardianship, as many people now refer to it, is not only a joy, it is a serious responsibility. During the years, your companion will rely on you for love, attention, proper nutrition, training, and good health care. To satisfy these requirements, you must be prepared for the financial aspects of responsible pet ownership as well as for the investments you cannot really measure: time and emotion.

The Best Time to Acquire a Lhasa Apso

If you have made your decision and your heart is set on a Lhasa Apso, you need to think about the best time to introduce one into your life and your home. You may want a Lhasa Apso right now, but there may be other circumstances that prevent you from fulfilling this dream immediately. It is not always easy to find the perfect dog right away. Start contacting breeders now so you can be placed on their waiting lists. Sometimes it's hard to be patient, but in the end you will find a Lhasa Apso that is ideal for you and you won't be disappointed.

Time to Spare

If you have too many obligations and your free time is limited, you should postpone your purchase until you have the time to give your Lhasa the care and attention it deserves. Lhasa Apsos are bright, active, and protective. They thrive on your company and affection, and may become bored when left all alone, especially for long periods of time. Bored dogs and puppies often get into mischief and that's when good dogs turn bad. If your Lhasa has nothing to do and you aren't there to keep it company, it can develop unwanted behaviors, including barking, chewing, digging, and destroying objects.

If you are moving or changing jobs, a new pet can be added stress rather than enjoyment. If you are planning a vacation soon, you will have to make arrangements for animal care in your absence. Rather than stress your new companion by a change in environment and caregivers, it is best to wait until you return from vacation before you introduce a new dog into your home.

Pups, Not Presents

We all have seen the movies, animations, and advertisements in which a young puppy is wrapped up in bows sitting by the fireplace as a surprise holiday gift. There are two things

wrong with this concept. First, it is unwise to buy a pet for someone else. Pet ownership is a responsibility not everyone wants to assume. And if a person wants a new dog, it is a sure thing that person also would prefer to choose the animal, rather than have someone else make that decision. Second, adding a new pet to the family during the holiday season should be discouraged. This is a time when most people already have more than enough to do with visitors and commitments. New pets often are overlooked in the busy holiday shuffle with all the distractions and excitement. Families cannot take the time out during the holidays to learn about, supervise, socialize, and care for a new animal. Visitors and guests may stress, frighten, or mishandle the new dog. They may even be bitten. Someone may forget to close the kennel, a door, or a fence gate and your new friend may escape, be lost or injured, or even killed by a moving vehicle. In the holiday confusion, your pet could miss a meal, or be overfed, unless someone is specifically assigned the responsibility of feeding. Finally, dogs purchased and transported (especially in cold weather) during the holidays may be more stressed or prone to illness than usual. To prevent stress to yourself and to your new canine companion, wait until the holidays are over before you bring it home.

Household Pets

Your Lhasa Apso ("Lily") is full of energy and curiosity. She has a keen sense of smell and is interested in meeting all the new members of your family, including other household pets. Make sure the introductions are done slowly and safely. For example, if you own another dog

Lhasa puppies enjoy playmates. This Pekingese puppy (on left) is just about the right size!

or a cat, don't expect them to be friends at the onset. Your other pets will be cautious and possibly jealous of the newcomer. A resentful cat can inflict serious injury on an unsuspecting dog, especially a tiny puppy. Eye injuries from cat scratches are common accidents experienced by dogs. And if you have another dog in the home, remember that it may be jealous of the attention you are giving the newcomer, particularly if your dog is an adult or aged animal. Even if your pets are happy to have Lily join the family, be sure that they do not play too roughly and accidentally injure her. Adult

Lhasa Apsos served as guardians of imperial families of Tibet and China for hundreds of years. Lhasas are courageous, bold, protective, and devoted.

With good care and proper nutrition, your Lhasa can live 15 years or more.

Lhasa Apsos may be hardy, sturdy little dogs, but a tiny puppy can be very fragile.

Making Introductions

A good way to start introductions in the family is to place Lily in an area of the home where she is safe from other animals, but where they can observe and smell each other. For example, if you have a laundry area, or space next to the kitchen, you can place a baby barrier gate to prevent the new arrival from running loose in the house without your permission until she adapts to her new environment and your other pets are used to her. Make sure the barrier has a mesh small enough to prevent escape or accidental injury or Lily

Lhasas love to explore.

Your Lhasa Apso will eagerly look forward to your return. When you are home, your Lhasa will warn you of approaching visitors.

Even a puppy has the instinct to destroy prey! Small pets and birds sense when there is a predator in the area and will be frightened and stressed if their cage is approached. Lhasa Apsos are very clever and very quick! Make sure the lid or door to your small pet's cage is securely fastened. Then place the cage where Lily cannot find it. Remember, she has a very keen sense of smell and will easily find these animals, so don't just place them out of sight—make sure they are out of reach!

becoming trapped in it. You may also put Lily in her crate the first few evenings so that your other household animals can approach and investigate, but cannot harm her. Remember to pay extra attention to your established pets so they are not jealous. It will be a real challenge juggling your attentions among your pets and spreading your affection so that they all feel they have received their fair share!

In most cases, animals learn to live together peacefully in a household. If your new Lhasa Apso is aggressive toward other dogs, neutering (spaying or castrating) your dogs will help the problem. The results are best if your pet is neutered at a young age.

Friends or Foes?

There are some household pets Lily should never meet. These include any small mammals (such as mice, rats, hamsters, guinea pigs, rabbits, or ferrets), birds, or reptiles. Instinct will tell Lily that these small animals are fair game.

Should Your Lhasa Apso Be Neutered?

Lhasa Apsos thrive with tender loving care, exercise, proper nutrition, and preventive veterinary care. One of the most important health decisions you will make is whether to have Lily spayed, or, if you have a male Lhasa Apso ("Lotus"), to have him castrated. These procedures (called "gonadectomy" or "neutering") refer to the inactivation or removal of some, or all, of the tissues in the body associated with reproduction (testicles in the male, ovaries and uterus in the female).

Spaying

Female Lhasas usually come into estrus (also called "in heat" or "in season") around the age of six months and cycle approximately every six months thereafter, depending on their family genetics. Ideally, your female should be spayed before her first estrous cycle, and certainly before her second estrous cycle, so that she will have a significantly reduced chance of developing mammary (breast) cancer later in life. If you wait until after the second estrous cycle, your pet will have almost as much of a chance of developing breast cancer as if she had not been spayed. Mammary cancer is common in older dogs, and 50 percent of mammary cancer in dogs is life-threatening. So, it makes good medical sense to spay your pet at a very early age.

Neutering

Early neutering can be performed safely on pups between 6 and 16 weeks of age. Studies have shown that prepubertal gonadectomy does not affect growth rate, food intake, or weight gain of growing dogs. In 1993, the American Veterinary Medical Association formally approved early neutering of dogs (and cats), a procedure many veterinarians and humane organizations have been promoting for years.

There are distinct health advantages for dogs that are neutered early in life:

1. Significantly reduces the chance of developing mammary (breast) cancer if the ovaries are removed before the female's second, and preferably first, estrous cycle

2. Prevents ovarian, uterine, testicular, or epididymal diseases, such as cancer and infection

3. Prevents unwanted pregnancies

4. Less surgical procedure time required

5. Rapid recovery period (young, healthy animals heal quickly)

6. Fewer behavior problems

7. Eliminates the inconveniences associated with a female dog in estrus (vaginal bleeding and discharge that can stain furniture and carpets and attract neighborhood dogs)

No procedure is completely without risk or side effects. Your veterinarian will advise you about the benefits and possible risks of neutering your pet.

Lhasas enjoy each other's company. If you add a new puppy to your family, be sure to give your adult Lhasa more love and attention than usual, so it will know it is still the "top dog" and it won't be jealous of the new arrival.

SELECTING YOUR LHASA APSO

The best way to find a Lhasa Apso is to begin with your local or national breed association. These associations will provide a list of reputable Lhasa Apso breeders. You may also join a breed, or all-breed, dog club in your area where you can meet breeders, dog trainers, and professional dog show handlers who can provide a wealth of information about various breeders.

Where to Find a Lhasa Apso

Dog publications, available from your local bookstore or pet store, contain numerous advertisements placed by dog breeders with animals for sale.

Be sure to purchase from a reputable breeder. Don't be surprised if the breeder you select does not have puppies immediately available. Just remember that a good Lhasa Apso is well worth the wait. If you are certain you want to be the proud owner of a Lhasa Apso, it is not too early to start checking with breeders today.

If you are not going to breed Lhasa Apsos, have your pet neutered. Early neutering has many health advantages.

Puppy or Adult?

Whether you choose to raise a puppy or adopt an adolescent or adult dog will depend on your personal preferences and home situation. Most people want to start with a puppy, because they want to integrate it into their family at an early age, and because puppies are so cute. But a puppy isn't a puppy for long, so if you have the opportunity to purchase a wonderful, well-mannered adolescent or adult dog, you might want to give it some serious thought.

When purchasing any dog, the most important considerations are the animal's health, temperament, and personality. A dog's personality is well established by the time it is 8 to 12 weeks of age. By obtaining Lotus in the very early stages of life, you may positively influence his adult personality and behavior development. This is much easier than trying to change an established undesirable behavior in an adult dog. However, sometimes, for a variety of reasons, a breeder may have an adolescent or young adult dog available for sale. If the dog has been well socialized as a youngster and well trained, there are many advantages to purchasing an older dog. You can skip the trials and tribulations of puppyhood, including housebreaking, leash training, and basic discipline (such as training your pet not to bark, not to chew on your belongings, and not to dig up your garden). You must be certain, however, that you and the dog are a good match. It is not unreasonable to request a brief trial period when you purchase an adult dog, so that you can be sure the animal will successfully adapt to a new family and change of lifestyle.

An older, well-trained Lhasa Apso may be more expensive than a puppy. This is because the older the dog, the more time, effort, and expense the breeder has invested in it. No matter what price you pay for your pet, just keep in mind that it will be insignificant compared to the costs you will incur in feeding, grooming supplies, toys, housing, and veterinary care during the animal's lifetime. So save your money, take your time, and invest in the best.

Selecting a Puppy

The first rule in selecting a puppy is to take your time. Don't rush into things and don't be an impulse buyer. It is easy to fall in love with the first (and every!) puppy you see, but don't buy the puppy because it is "cute," or because you "felt sorry for it." You risk ending up with an animal that may have serious medical or behavioral problems. Do your homework, take your time, and use your head before your heart. The best way to stay on the right track and increase your chances of finding a well-socialized, well-bred, healthy Lhasa puppy is to buy from a reputable breeder.

Visiting Breeders

Once you have located a breeder with animals available for sale, make an appointment to see the puppies in person. Be sure to verify that they have been registered and ask for a copy of their parents' registration papers. The breeder can also provide you with a copy of the puppies' pedigree(s). Ask the breeder if the parents have additional certifications, for example, registration by the Canine Eye Registration Foundation (CERF), or any type of testing for freedom from inherited health problems.

Watch Lotus in his home environment at the breeder's. Is he happy and outgoing? Is he alert and active, playful and curious? Carefully observe Lotus and his littermates for signs of good health and strong personalities. A Lhasa Apso is bright, confident, and eager to investigate. After he has had some time to get to

Underneath all that hair is a well-developed muscular system. Lhasa Apsos are agile and strong in relation to their size.

CHECKLIST

Puppy Health

Attitude	Healthy, alert, playful, inquisitive
Eyes	Bright, clear, free of discharge
Ears	Clean, free of dirt and wax buildup, no evidence of head-shaking or scratching
Mouth	Gums bright pink, teeth properly aligned or slightly undershot
Skin and coat	Healthy, thick coat, well-groomed, free of knots and mats, and with no evidence of parasites or sores
Body condition	May seem a little plump, but should not have a distended belly or thin body
Movement	Normal gait for a puppy may seem a bit bouncy and sometimes clumsy

know you, Lotus should be friendly and playful. He should not be aggressive or shy.

Examining Pups

Check Lotus's eyes, ears, mouth, skin, coat, and movement. The eyes should be clear and bright and the ears should be clean. Normal gums are bright pink in color. Make sure all the teeth are present and that the baby (deciduous) teeth have fallen out where the adult teeth have replaced them. Sometimes the baby teeth do not come out and when the adult teeth grow in there are simply too many teeth in the mouth. Retained deciduous teeth need to be extracted. There should never be more than one tooth of the same type in the mouth at one time! In other words, if Lotus has a baby canine tooth and an adult canine tooth, the baby tooth needs to be removed right away so that the teeth grow in correctly and are not over-

crowded in the mouth. Ideally, Lotus's teeth should be in correct alignment; however, a slightly undershot bite (the lower jaw protrudes slightly outward past the upper jaw) is normal for a Lhasa Apso.

Check that the skin and coat are healthy and free of parasites or sores. The coat should be groomed and free of knots and mats. Look under the tail to be sure the area is clean and free of signs of blood or diarrhea.

Conscientious breeders are concerned about placing their puppies in caring, responsible homes. A breeder may ask you questions about your future plans for the puppy and the kind of home life the puppy will have. This is also your opportunity to ask questions, so take advantage of it.

Finally, ask to see Lotus's littermates again, and his parents, if they are available. This will help you determine their personalities and give

When selecting a Lhasa Apso, take your time and invest in the best. The perfect Lhasa for you is well worth the wait—and worth its weight in gold!

you a good idea of how you might expect Lotus to look and behave when he is an adult. Remember that the way you raise and handle Lotus, and the things he is exposed to as a youngster, will have a big influence on the way his character and temperament develop. Try to introduce him to people and different sights and sounds while he is still young and can adapt easily. The time you spend socializing Lotus as a puppy will pay off a thousandfold when he is a well-adjusted adult.

Male or Female?

If you are looking for a wonderful companion that will keep you entertained and be a faithful guardian, then either a male or female Lhasa Apso will do very well. The choice is based solely on personal preference.

Males are 10 to 11 inches (25.4 to 28 cm) at the shoulder and females are slightly smaller. Some people think that females are a bit more affectionate and gentler than males and that males are more assertive, strong-willed, and dominant. Some of this behavior depends not only on the animal's individual personality, but also on the type of socialization and treatment it received as a very young puppy. With training, kindness, patience, and understanding, either a male or female Lhasa Apso can fit nicely into the right family situation.

If you are thinking of raising Lhasa Apsos in the future, then you have to seriously consider your options and discuss these plans with the

Whether you are showing your pet off in the ring or in the neighborhood, take the time to groom your companion regularly so it always looks its best.

breeder, who can assist you in making an appropriate decision about which animal to purchase at the onset. Most novice breeders begin by investing in the best female they can find, often an adult that has proven herself in the showring and/or previously produced a litter. Then, with the help of an experienced breeder, the novice finds the most suitable stud dog for the female and pays for its services.

If you are not planning on breeding Lhasa Apsos, you definitely should have your dog, male or female, neutered as early as possible, for reasons previously discussed.

Show Dog or Companion Animal?

Decide if you want a top-notch show dog for breeding and exhibiting in dog show competitions, or if you are primarily interested in a Lhasa as a companion and household pet. A show dog must conform to certain breed standards, such as height, conformation, and character. A companion Lhasa may have minor imperfections with regard to the high conformation standards of a future champion, but be wonderful in all other respects. Usually, these differences are slight and can only be detected by the trained eye of a breeder or show judge. They in no way diminish the animal's value as a loving member of the family.

If you have decided that you want a show dog, be prepared to pay more for it than you would for a pet-quality companion. Also, keep

You'll know the right puppy when you see it! It's the most healthy, friendly, and playful one. It takes a special liking to you and seems to say, "Take me home!"

Either a male or a female Lhasa Apso makes a wonderful companion. You may decide to have one of each!

TIP

Important Questions to Ask the Seller

1 Are the pups registered with the kennel club?

2 How old are the pups and what sexes are available?

3 At what age were the pups weaned?

4 How many pups were in the litter?

5 Have the pups received any inoculations? If so, which ones?

6 Have the pups been wormed or tested for worms?

7 Have the pups had their eyes examined by a veterinary ophthalmologist? If so, ask to see the eye certification.

8 Have the pups been handled frequently and are they socialized?

9 Have the pups received any basic training (housebreaking, leash training)?

10 What kind of food are the pups eating at this time?

11 Ask for a 48-hour health guarantee until you can have the puppy examined by your own veterinarian.

12 Ask to see the parents and littermates of the pup.

in mind that although the parents may be champion show dogs, there is no guarantee that the puppy will turn out to be a champion, too. If you are serious about purchasing a show dog, the best advice is to buy an adult animal that already has been successful in the show ring. Even the loveliest puppy can change as it grows up and may not reach the show potential you had hoped for. If you buy a puppy as a show prospect, you are guessing that the animal will attain a certain level of conformational quality after it has completed all its development and growth phases. A lot of changes can take place between puppyhood and adulthood. When you buy an adult, what you see is what you get and there is no guesswork involved.

Age and Longevity

It is a fact that small dog breeds live longer than large breeds, and the Lhasa Apso is no exception. Lhasa Apsos are hardy dogs and with good nutrition and loving care they may live 15 years or more. This is another reason to be particular when choosing your companion. Dog ownership is a long-term commitment.

Pedigree and Registration

Before making a final decision and completing the sale, be sure the puppy's health records, pedigree, and registration papers are in order. A puppy should have a health certificate signed by a veterinarian stating that the puppy has been examined and is in good health and able to travel. Dates of inoculations and any medications (such as worming medication) should be noted on the health certificate. Your veterinarian will need this information to set up a preventive health care program for your pet.

One of the many pleasures of owning a purebred dog is pride of ownership and the variety of activities in which you and your companion can participate. For example, without registration papers, there is no proof of parentage or lineage. When you purchase Lotus, be sure to verify that both of his parents are registered and that he has been registered as well. Do not confuse official registration with a pedigree. A pedigree is not an official document. It is a chart showing the ancestral tree of the puppy. A pedigree is prepared by the breeder, listing the dam and sire and their relatives. It does not guarantee that your dog is registered with the kennel club (see Information, page 92). Registration is an official document issued by the kennel club that is proof that your dog is purebred.

You should receive application papers from the breeder to register the puppy in your name. Once you choose a name for the puppy, complete the application form and mail it to the kennel club address on the application with the appropriate registration fee. You will then receive a certificate of registration from the kennel club, listing you as the owner.

If you purchase your Lhasa Apso as a young puppy born in the United States, the breeder will give you one of the following American Kennel Club (AKC) forms:

Registration Application

This is a blue slip of paper that indicates the breeder, the litter registration number, the litter birth date, and the names and registration numbers of your dog's parents. There are spaces to write in the dog's name, for the breeder to sign transfer of ownership, and for you to sign as the new owner. Some breeders require their kennel name to be included as part of the dog's name. The breeder can name the puppies before they are sold or elect to have the new owners name them. Once the registration application is completed, the new owner sends it to the AKC, with the appropriate fee (indicated on the application form). The new owner then receives either a full registration or a limited registration (see below).

Full Registration

This white slip of paper has a purple border and shows the registered name and number of the dog, its birth date, breed, and color. The breeder and owner are also indicated. This type of registration allows for participation in AKC competitions and events, as well as the ability to register future offspring of the animal with the AKC.

Limited Registration

This form looks exactly like a full registration certificate, except the border is orange. It provides the same documentation as a full registration certificate. However, puppies born from animals with limited registration cannot be registered with the AKC. Only the breeder, not the owner, can change an animal's status from limited to full registration.

AT HOME WITH YOUR LHASA APSO

You have found the perfect Lhasa Apso! Now you are eager to bring her home and make her feel comfortable and secure. Part of your pet's success in adapting to her new family and her new life depends on making sure you are well prepared for the new arrival.

Prepare your house and yard *before* bringing the new puppy home, because once the puppy arrives, everyone will be caught up in all the excitement of the new arrival!

First of all, make sure your house and yard are safe. Check for holes in and under the fence and remove objects in the house that can present a serious health hazard (see Safety First, page 28).

If you have everything that you both will need ready in advance, the transition period will go smoothly.

Your Lhasa Apso Comes Home

Dogs are creatures of habit, so any change in their daily routine or environment is poten-

At last! You have found the perfect Lhasa puppy! This cuddly, soft ball of fur will grow into a brave guardian and a lifelong friend.

tially stressful to them. Don't expect everything to go perfectly the first few days your new companion is home with you. Whether you bring home a puppy or an adult dog, there will be a period of adjustment of a few days before your pet will feel settled in and secure.

Settling In

The "settling in" period is very important. It sets the tone for the future relationship you and your Lhasa will establish. The lifelong bond that you will enjoy with your pet starts from the day she comes home. As you teach your new friend about proper behavior, feeding, and sleeping arrangements, remember—patience, kindness, and consistency will be your three most valuable virtues.

Ideally, your new acquisition will have been introduced to a travel kennel before you bring her home. A travel kennel makes an ideal portable doghouse for Lhasa Apsos, so this is an item that you will use frequently, for travel and home. If Lily has a favorite toy or blanket, ask

TIP

Supplies for Your New Lhasa Apso
- ✔ Food and water dishes
- ✔ Quality puppy/dog food
- ✔ Comfortable sleeping quarters (dog bed, doghouse, designated area in home)
- ✔ Travel kennel
- ✔ Identification tag
- ✔ Collar
- ✔ Leash
- ✔ Grooming supplies (slicker brush, wide-toothed metal comb, stripping knife, hound's glove, blunt-tipped scissors, nail trimmers, styptic powder, gentle emollient shampoo, ear cleaning solution)
- ✔ Dental supplies (toothbrush, dentifrice)
- ✔ First aid kit
- ✔ Exercise pen (X-pen), safety gate, or some type of enclosure
- ✔ Toys

the breeder if you can place it in the travel kennel for the trip home. A familiar item will help her feel more secure during the trip and during the next few days in her new environment.

Place the familiar item, or a soft blanket or towel, in the travel kennel on top of a layer of shredded newspaper. Make sure Lily has not eaten for the last two hours so that she is less likely to become carsick and vomit. The trip home may be the first time she has ever traveled in a car. If she feels queasy, she may drool excessively, so be sure to bring along plenty of paper towels. Allow Lily to relieve herself before you place her in the travel kennel.

Your new companion may protest all the way home, or she may simply sleep. Make a decision right now not to give in to her crying, no matter how difficult it is. Talk to her soothingly, but be forewarned! If you hold her on your lap for the trip home, she will not forget it, and she will expect you to allow her on your lap during every car trip you take together. When she is an adult she will be larger. It is safer for both of you if she remains in her travel kennel whenever she travels in the car.

When you arrive home, give Lily a small drink of water. Remember that she is probably fatigued from her trip and all the excitement, so a little quiet time is in order. If she is sleepy, allow her to rest. If she feels like becoming acquainted, do so calmly and gently. Avoid loud noises and sudden movements. Be sure to teach any children in the home to respect Lily's space and privacy. Teach them the proper way to lift and handle her, by gently putting one hand under the chest and the other under the hindquarters for support. Never lift a Lhasa Apso by the scruff of the neck or by the limbs. Small children should remain seated on the floor when petting or handling a puppy, to prevent dropping or injury.

Naming Your Lhasa Apso

The first thing your Lhasa Apso will need to learn is her name. Once she knows her name, you can get her attention and start a line of communication—the first step in her lifelong training.

Your dog's personality will shine through at the onset, so you will most likely have no difficulty thinking of a name that suits your companion and her character. If you need some

Convenient Housing Options

Travel kennel	Ideal for use as a small doghouse; lightweight, easy to clean, well-ventilated; provides privacy
Exercise pens (X-pens)	Portable, folding pens, available in a variety of sizes, with attachments for dishes
Doghouse	Should be constructed of nonporous material, easy to clean and disinfect
Safety gates	Useful for closing off a designated area or stairway to prevent escape or injury
Bedding	Bedding should be natural material (cotton, wool) because synthetic materials, or bedding containing cedar shavings, may cause allergies

ideas, you will find plenty in dog magazines and books of baby names.

It seems easier for dogs to recognize names with two syllables. This avoids confusion later on when you give one-syllable commands, such as *"Sit," "Stay,"* and *"Down."*

When you have selected a name, use it often when talking to your new pet. When she responds or comes to you, praise her lavishly. It won't take her long to know who she is.

Housing Considerations

A Lhasa Apso may have a thick coat to protect it from harsh weather, but historically the breed has been kept for centuries as an indoor pet. Your Lhasa will love to play outside, but she prefers indoor living and sharing the same creature comforts you enjoy.

Be gentle when handling a young puppy. Always support the back by placing a hand underneath the hindquarters.

Sleeping Quarters

When you bring Lily home, decide on a safe place (an X-pen, laundry room, area off the kitchen) where she can feel secure and have some privacy, yet be observed. Ideally, this area will be Lily's permanent housing and sleeping quarters. Take her to her new den to explore and relax for several minutes. Feed her a little treat and praise her. Lily should associate her

At first your pup may seem a bit shy, but once it gets to know you, its distinct personality will shine through and you will think of a name that suits your little friend perfectly!

space with enjoyment. It should be a pleasant place to be. Make sure she can also observe the household activities so she doesn't feel isolated. Lhasa Apsos are intelligent, active dogs and they enjoy being a central part of everything going on around them. Exposure to various sights, sounds, smells, activities, and people is an important part of socializing a dog. Remember that Lily doesn't know the rules yet and will require training, so make sure her den is in an area where she cannot chew furniture or urinate on the carpet. Later, when you have started training her, do not use her sleeping quarters as a place to go when she is punished. Her territory should always be a comforting place where she goes when all is right with the world, and not when she is in trouble.

If you have acquired an older Lhasa Apso, try to duplicate its previous housing situation as much as possible to reduce the stress of changing environments.

Safety First

Lily will be very curious and interested in learning more about her new home. Some of the characteristics you admire most about your dog—her intelligence, small size, and activity level—also create some of the biggest problems for her safety and make her prone to accidents. Believe it or not, there are countless life-threatening situations in your cozy home. Be sure that you have removed any potential hazards before you let Lily explore and be sure that she is supervised at all times.

Household Cleaning Products and Chemicals

Cleaning products and chemicals are potentially deadly for Lily if she comes in contact with them. Some types of paints can be toxic if she chews on wooden baseboards or walls.

Be sure to keep the seat and lid down on the toilet. Many dogs will drink from the toilet and if you use any cleaning chemicals in the toilet tank, these can be very harmful.

Antifreeze

Antifreeze (ethylene glycol) is a major cause of animal poisoning. This common chemical can be found on garage floors. It has a sweet taste that attracts animals. Only a very small amount is required to cause severe kidney damage. Survival depends on an early diagnosis. If you suspect your car is leaking antifreeze, do not allow any pets in the garage.

There is now a type of antifreeze on the market that is said to be nontoxic to animals, so you may want to see if this product is available in your area.

Rodent Poisons and Snap Traps

If you have any rodent bait that has been left out for wild vermin, pick it up immediately. It is as deadly for Lily as it is for the wild rodents. If there are any dead rodents in the garage or yard that may have been poisoned, discard them. Lhasa Apsos are curious and investigate anything they find. If Lily eats a poisoned animal, she can be poisoned as well.

If you have snap traps set in your house or garage, remove them. They can break small toes or injure a nose.

Electrical Shock

Electrocution from gnawing on an electrical cord is a real potential danger that could cost Lily her life, and possibly cause an electrical fire.

Kitchens and Appliances

It is not uncommon for pets to be burned from hot liquids that have spilled from pots on the stove, or from a hot iron falling on them from the ironing board after a tangle in the electrical cord. Before you do the laundry, check the dryer. Incredibly, many small pets have been found, too late, inside the dryer, where they had settled in for a cozy snooze.

Your Lhasa will lay its head anywhere comfortable, especially if it is close to you! If you allow your pup to sleep on your bed or furniture, it will expect to have the same privileges when it is an adult!

Doors

Make sure all doors to the outside or the garage are closed. If Lily escapes outdoors, she can become lost or may be the victim of an automobile accident. To prevent a broken tail or toes, be certain Lily is not in the way when you close doors.

Injuries

Everyone in the house must pay close attention to where they step. Lhasa Apsos are small and move quickly. Lily can dart out from under the furniture, be underfoot before you know it, and be stepped on and injured. If you try to sidestep her, you can also be injured if you lose your balance, trip, or fall.

Poisonous Plants

Many ornamental plants are toxic to animals, including philodendron, dieffenbachia, foxglove, and lily of the valley. Keep household plants out of reach and limit home and garden plants to nontoxic varieties.

A fenced-in yard provides an excellent place for exercise. Make sure there are no holes in or under the fence and that the gate is securely fastened.

overdose of common medicines, including aspirin, acetaminophen (Tylenol), and ibuprofen (Motrin, Advil), can be fatal for her. Chocolate contains a methylxanthine substance, similar to caffeine, called theobromine that is toxic to dogs. Hard candies can become lodged between the teeth at the back of the jaw or in the throat and become a serious choking hazard.

Foreign Objects

Dogs explore with their mouths and often will eat anything, even if it doesn't taste very good. Make sure small balls, children's toys, rubber bands, paper clips, pens, sewing needles, and anything else you can think of are out of Lily's reach. Coins are a particular hazard because pennies contain high levels of zinc and can cause zinc poisoning. Be sure that any toys you purchase are safe and do not contain small pieces, bells, or whistles that may be a choking hazard.

Garbage

As unappealing as it may seem to us, all dogs insist on exploring garbage cans. In addition to the obvious hazards associated with this activity, dogs may also suffer from "garbage poisoning," a form of poisoning caused by bacteria and bacterial toxins found in old and decaying foods.

Candies and Medicines

Make sure you have not left any foods or medicine containers within Lily's reach. An

Identification

The very first thing you should do once you have brought your new companion home is to be sure she is properly identified. If Lily ever becomes lost, your chances of being reunited are very slim without proper identification. Ninety percent of all lost family pets are unidentifiable and 70 percent of these animals never return home. Annually, 20 million lost American pets are euthanized. Don't let Lily become one of the statistics. If she doesn't yet have identification, stop whatever you are doing and see to it right now. You'll be glad you did.

Microchips

One of the most recent, high-tech, and efficient forms of animal identification is by means of a microchip. A microchip is a microtransponder the size of a grain of rice that is implanted under the skin quickly and easily by injection. The microchip has a series of numbers unique to itself so that each animal has its own identification number. A handheld scanner (also called a decoder or reader) is used to read the identification number. Microchips are safe, permanent, and tamper-proof. The entire identification procedure (microchip implant or scanning) takes only a few seconds. Scanning is absolutely painless and accurate.

Once a microchip has been implanted in an animal, the following information is entered into a central computer registry: the animal's identification number, a description of the animal, the owner's name, address, and telephone number, and an alternate contact in case the owner cannot be reached. It is the owner's responsibility to update the registry in the event of a change in information. An identification tag for the animal's collar is also provided, indicating the animal's identification number and the registry's telephone number.

Lost animals can be identified at animal shelters, humane societies, and veterinary offices. Once the animal's identification number is displayed, the central registry is contacted and the owner's information is released for contact.

Surprisingly, the cost for all of this technology, including the microchip and its implantation, is modest. In addition, the price for lifetime enrollment in the American Kennel Club Animal Recovery database is currently only $12.50. For the life of your pet, this is an investment you cannot afford to ignore.

Collars and Nametags

Every dog needs a collar and a leash. These are the essential pieces of equipment for training and restraining your pet. A collar also serves as a piece of identification. If your pet wears a wide, flat, nylon collar, you can write your name and phone number on it. If a light nylon or leather collar is used, you can have a nametag engraved to attach to it. Many local pet stores offer on-the-spot nametag engraving. Collars and tags are easily visible and let others know your lost companion has a family.

Slip or choke collars are inappropriate for Lhasas unless they have been trained to this type of collar. Never leave your pet unattended wearing a slip or choke collar. They can accidentally catch or hang on objects and your pet could strangle to death.

Tattoos

Tattoos are a good form of identification because they are permanent. However, they are not a good identification alternative for Lhasa Apsos because it is difficult to tattoo several numbers on their inner thigh or belly, due to their small size.

Housebreaking Your Lhasa Apso

There is nothing difficult about housebreaking your Lhasa Apso. Because Lhasas are so smart and like to be very clean, housebreaking is usually accomplished quickly. What's the secret? Patience, diligence, consistency, making sure your puppy gets to the right place at the right time, and lots of praise.

Proper Technique

Lhasa Apsos are meticulous about their living quarters and will do their best not to soil where they are housed or confined. This is another excellent reason for keeping Lily in a travel kennel on the way home from the breeder's. If the trip is not too long, she probably will wait to urinate or defecate. You can start out right by taking her outside immediately upon arrival and

Collars and nametags are a better form of identification for Lhasas than tattoos. With all that hair and such a small body, it's difficult to see a tattoo!

Be sure there are no poisonous plants in the garden!

TIP

Housebreaking Tips

1 Start housebreaking your Lhasa the day she arrives—it is never too early.

2 Make sure your puppy is receiving good nutrition, has normal stools, and is free of internal parasites.

3 Keep your Lhasa on a regular feeding schedule.

4 Let your puppy outside several times a day, first thing in the morning, after every meal, after naps, and as late as possible in the evening.

5 Never scold your puppy if she has an accident.

6 Praise her profusely when she does the right thing.

7 Learn to recognize the signs when your puppy needs to go outside.

8 Be patient and understanding.

---

placing her right where you want her to learn to do her business. She will immediately urinate, and when she does, praise her repeatedly. You are off to a positive start.

Next, place Lily in her designated living area. This area should have easy-to-clean flooring, such as tile or linoleum, but no carpeting. Remember that she has a very small bladder

If you have a spa or swimming pool, keep them covered when you are not home. To help prevent accidental drowning, teach your Lhasa where the steps are and make a ramp so it can climb out—just in case it falls in while you are away.

Cleaning Up After "Accidents"

There are several carpet cleaning products designed specifically for removal of pet odors and stains. Some of these are available from your veterinarian or your local supermarket. However, if you don't have any of these commercial products immediately available, and if your puppy accidentally soils the carpet, you may use either

✔ a mixture of half vinegar (clear) and half water lightly dabbed on and blotted with a towel

or

✔ a small amount of club soda lightly dabbed on and blotted with a towel.

Remember to test a small section of your carpet first to be sure the solution does not damage it.

Holidays can be a dangerous time for pets! Be sure that chocolates, hard candies, small toys, choking hazards, electrical wires, and poisonous ornamental plants are out of your Lhasa's reach.

It won't take your Lhasa long to learn not to soil in the house. Pay close attention to your pup and take it to the right spot when it needs to go outside.

and does not have full control of bladder or bowels yet. She will need to go outside frequently and certainly will have a few accidents before she is fully trained. But remember that Lily wants to please. As soon as she understands that she should urinate or defecate only in the area you have indicated, she will try her best to wait until you take her to that spot. If she soils in her confinement, it is an accident, so don't punish her. The outdated and cruel training method of rubbing a dog's nose in its urine, or hitting a dog, is the worst thing you can do. Don't raise your voice or reprimand Lily. She will not associate your scolding with her natural body functions, especially if the scolding occurs long after the act of elimination. Lhasa Apsos are very sensitive and scolding a puppy that has an accident is a harsh, unreasonable treatment that may confuse her or break her spirit. If that happens, she may become depressed or less sociable, or withdraw from you. Everything is new and strange to her, and like a baby, she has little control over her elimination at this point.

When you have to be away, or during the night, confine your puppy to an area and cover the floor with newspapers. Your puppy will use the papers for its toilet until it is completely housebroken.

Rather, clean up the mess and work on positive reinforcement by praising her profusely when she does the right thing.

Be Attentive

Lily doesn't know how to tell you when she needs to go. For now, it is up to you to be attentive to her needs and signs of impending urination or defecation so you can take her outside in time. Signs include sniffing the ground, pacing, circling, whining, crying, and acting anxious. You must act fast as soon as this behavior begins or you will be too late! Lily will always need to urinate immediately after waking up from a nap or after eating a meal, so in these instances, take her directly outside without waiting for signs. Remember to lavish praise on her for her performance.

Ideally, a young puppy should be let outside every few hours. Of course, there will be times when you simply cannot be available to do this. When you have to be out of the house, or during the night, keep Lily restricted to a designated, confined area and cover the floor of the area with newspapers. She will do her best to urinate and defecate on the papers. Now she has the right idea and is learning to control her elimination until she reaches a given spot, even if it isn't yet the backyard.

The Adolescent Lhasa Apso

When Lily is a little older, you can restrict her to her travel kennel for brief periods of time

Frequent brushing is necessary to keep the Lhasa Apso's long coat in optimal condition.

when you have to be away. Lhasas will not soil their "den," so when you return, be sure to take Lily outside immediately. Don't use the travel crate for housebreaking, however, if you have to be away for extended periods of time.

Eventually Lily will be able to wait for longer periods of time as she develops more bowel and bladder control. It will be a while before she can wait until morning to urinate, but during that time she will use the newspapers you leave on the floor.

Housebreaking is the result of two-way communication. You teach Lily that she must eliminate outside, and she must find a way to let you know her desire to go outside when nature calls. She may never "ask" to go outside by barking or scratching at the door or fetching her leash like the dogs in the movies. But if she hasn't been outside for a long period of time, or has just woken up, or finished a meal, or started to pant and stare at you, you know what to do.

Grooming

One of the joys of owning a Lhasa Apso is showing it off at its best. Regular grooming will keep Lily's coat and skin in top condition and is an important part of her health care program. Grooming should always be a positive experience for Lily and an enjoyable activity for you. Many Lhasa Apso owners groom their dogs as a form of relaxation and artistic expression. It is a documented fact that people can lower their blood pressure simply by touching or caressing an animal. Lily also will benefit from the close human contact and the special attention she

receives during the grooming session. She will enjoy the massage sensation and skin stimulation a good brushing provides.

Grooming sessions are a good time to thoroughly check Lily for signs of dry or oily skin, lumps and bumps, parasites, stickers, scabs, knots, and mats. During the grooming sessions you should check Lily's eyes to be sure they are clear and bright. It is not unusual for Lhasas to

TIP

Grooming Pointers

✔ Keep grooming sessions brief and always end on a positive note.
✔ When Lily requires a reprimand, use the word *"No"* consistently.
✔ Never use Lily's name in connection with a reprimand.
✔ Always praise her for good performance and behavior.
✔ Train by using positive reinforcement (praise or food rewards) and not by negative reinforcement (scolding, physical punishment).

suffer from eye irritation due to long hairs coming in contact with, or sticking to, the eyes. Take this opportunity to trim away stray hairs that may be a problem. If Lily's eyes frequently tear, contact your veterinarian.

Prolonged tearing can stain the hair around the inner corners of the eyes a dark reddish brown color. Your veterinarian can provide you with a product developed specifically for use around the eyes that can help eliminate the stain, but more important, your veterinarian can determine the cause of tearing and treat it appropriately before it becomes a serious problem.

Many Lhasa owners delegate most of the grooming to a professional. If you do not have the time, or are not inclined to learn proper grooming techniques, this is a good choice. If you enjoy doing the work yourself, here are a few tips to make the grooming session a safe and enjoyable experience for you and your pet:

1. Remember that several short training sessions are better than one long one. Limit puppy grooming to 3 to 5 minutes. Puppies have short attention spans and bore or tire easily.

2. Begin training for grooming as soon as possible.

3. Designate an area to use exclusively for grooming. This should be an easy-to-clean, convenient location, close to an electrical outlet (for hair dryer, clippers, electric nail files, or vacuum cleaner).

4. Select a table that is high enough for you to work at a comfortable height, depending on whether you prefer to work sitting or standing.

5. Make sure the table surface is nonslip to prevent falls or injury.

6. Invest in the best. Purchase quality tools and equipment, particularly brushes, combs, scissors (blunt-tipped and thinning), and nail

Patience, consistency, and praise are the keys to successful training. Your pet will try its best to please you.

It is not unusual in Lhasas for the bottom incisors to be slightly undershot (protrude slightly).

clippers. This will reduce your chances of developing blisters on your fingers, or sore wrists and arms from overexertion.

7. Place all the grooming items near the grooming table, within easy reach.

8. Use only products designed for dogs to ensure a pH balance for canine skin, including emollient shampoos or spray-on dry shampoos.

9. Give a small food reward at the conclusion of each grooming session and take your pet for a walk afterward, whenever possible. Your dog will associate grooming with other pleasant experiences and look forward to the next grooming session.

10. Never leave any animal unattended on the table.

The time and effort you invest in Lily's coat and skin will keep her looking in top condition. As you become more familiar with the Lhasa Apso standard and develop more skill at grooming, you will find ways to groom Lily so that you can enhance her features to more closely reflect the ideal Lhasa Apso.

Dental Care

Regular dental care and toothbrushing are very important aspects of Lily's health care program and should start when she is still a puppy.

Puppies, like babies, are born without teeth. When Lhasas reach three to four weeks of age, their deciduous teeth (baby teeth) emerge. At around 4 months, these 28 temporary

TIP

Bad Breath

Bad breath is not normal for a dog. If your Lhasa has bad breath, she may have periodontal disease. Contact your veterinarian right away.

Proper nutrition plays an important role in your pet's dental health. Bad breath can mean your pet has teeth and gum problems.

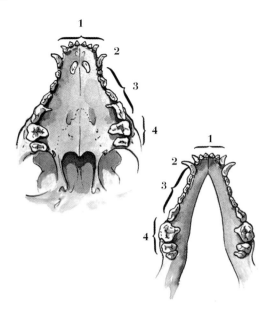

The Lhasa Apso's permanent teeth.
Upper teeth: 1. incisors (six) 2. canines
(two) 3. premolars (eight) 4. molars (four).
Lower teeth: 1. incisors (six) 2. canines
(two) 3. premolars (eight) 4. molars (six).

teeth begin to fall out and are replaced with 42 permanent teeth. During this time, puppies want to chew on everything, just like a baby who is teething, and it is important to provide your pet with lots of safe chew toys. By the time Lily is six months old, she will have all of her adult teeth. These teeth must last her a lifetime, so it is important to take good care of them by preventing plaque and tartar buildup and periodontal disease.

Fighting Plaque

Plaque is coating on the teeth caused by a combination of bacteria, saliva, and decaying food. As plaque builds up, a cement-like substance called tartar develops, usually starting at the gum line. It is yellow to brown in color and can eventually spread to cover the entire tooth. Periodontal disease develops as bacteria infect the root of the tooth and cause erosion of the surrounding bone that secures the tooth. Eventually, the root is destroyed and the tooth will fall out, or require extraction. Periodontal disease causes more problems than bad breath; swollen, painful, bleeding gums; and tooth loss. The bacteria present in the mouth and gums can enter the bloodstream and grow on the heart valves, causing heart problems, or infect the kidneys and other organs of the body.

The best way to reduce plaque buildup is dental brushing. It is easy to get Lily used to the idea of regular brushing when she is a puppy. Her baby teeth are good for practice and training. By the time her adult teeth are in, she will be used to the daily routine.

Check you Lhasa's teeth regularly for tartar and plaque buildup.

Brushing Your Lhasa's Teeth

Purchase a soft-bristle toothbrush and dog toothpaste recommended by your veterinarian or local pet store. Do not use human toothpaste. Many human products contain spearmint or peppermint or other substances that cause dogs to salivate (drool) profusely or that upset their stomachs. Use warm water. Cold water is unpleasant and may temporarily turn the gums and tongue bluish in color.

Start with the upper front teeth (incisors), brushing down and away from the gum line, and proceed back to the premolars and molars on one side of the mouth. You may also brush these teeth in a gentle, circular motion. Repeat on the upper teeth on the opposite side of the mouth. When you brush the bottom teeth, start with the incisors and work back to the molars, brushing up and away from the gum line. Repeat on the lower teeth on the opposite side of the mouth. Be patient. You may want to break the daily brushing into two sessions at the beginning. Spend about one minute on the upper teeth and then praise Lily for her good behavior. Later in the day you can spend another one-minute time increment on the bottom teeth, followed by profuse praise.

Good home dental care is a necessity, but it is not a replacement for veterinary dental visits. Even with the best of care, most dogs require routine professional dental cleaning and polishing.

Toenails

Lhasas need to have their toenails clipped occasionally, especially if they spend most of their time indoors and don't wear down their nails on hard surfaces. Check Lily's nails fre-

TIP

Foot Care

Here is a formula that you can mix and apply to your Lhasa Apso's feet to help toughen the footpads and dry sore lesions.

1 Boil 1 cup (240 ml) of water.

2 Steep 5 orange pekoe black tea bags in the water for 20 minutes.

3 Crush 5 aspirin tablets (325 mg each) and dissolve them in the tea solution.

4 Add 1/2 ounce (15 ml) of ethyl alcohol to the tea and aspirin solution and mix well.

5 Allow the mixture to cool.

6 Apply solution to affected areas of the footpads 3 to 4 times daily with a soft paintbrush until lesions are healed. (Do not use on raw or open lesions.)

7 Store in a tightly closed jar. The solution will keep for several months.

quently and don't let them become overgrown. She will probably need to have her nails trimmed once a month. You can ask your veterinarian or groomer to trim Lily's nails, or you can do it yourself.

Trimming

Toenail trimming is something most dog owners dread, but it really isn't difficult. If you

*Your Lhasa may appear to be dozing, but
under all that hair are watchful eyes that
don't miss a thing.*

*Your Lhasa will be a treasured family
member for many years.*

TIP

Treating Injuries

If you accidentally cut a toenail too
closely and you do not have styptic powder available, you may be able to stop
the bleeding by pushing the end of the
toenail into a piece of wax or a dry bar of
soap. This will serve as a plug until the
bleeding stops.

work with Lily's feet from the time she is very young, she will not mind having her feet handled and restrained. It is important to keep the nails trimmed so that they do not snag or tear, causing pain or discomfort. If the nails become too overgrown, they will eventually deform Lily's paws, interfere with her movement, and impede her ability to walk. In the most severe cases, overgrown toenails can curve under and pierce the footpads.

To determine if Lily requires a nail trim, stand her on the grooming table. None of the nails should touch the surface of the table. You will notice each toenail curves and tapers into a point. If the toenail is not too dark in color, you will be able to see pink inside the toenail; this is the "quick." This is the blood supply and just below it is the excess nail growth that you will remove. If Lily's toenails are too dark to differentiate where the quick ends, you can illuminate the nail with a penlight or a flashlight to find the line of demarcation where the blood supply ends.

There are different types of nail trimmers. Most Lhasa Apso owners prefer the guillotine-style clippers. To use these you place the toenail inside the metal loop, aligning the upper and lower blades with the area you wish to cut, and squeeze the clipper handles. A good rule of thumb is to cut only the very tip of the toenail. If the nail is still too long, continue to remove the end of the nail carefully in small increments. If you accidentally cut too close, you can stop the bleeding by applying styptic powder (a yellow clotting

Some Lhasa owners like to keep their pets coat trimmed, especially during warm weather. A ribbon accentuates this carefree "style."

A coat this gorgeous isn't created overnight! It is the result of regular grooming, attention to detail, good nutrition, and excellent health.

TIP

Exercise Precautions

✔ Remember to always keep your Lhasa Apso on a leash when you are exercising her in public. This act of responsible dog ownership will greatly reduce her chances of injury or becoming lost.

✔ Remember to be sensitive to your dog's needs. If she is panting excessively and having difficulty keeping up, stop exercising immediately! She may suffer from overexertion or heatstroke.

powder commercially available from your pet store or veterinarian) or by applying pressure to the toenail with a clean cloth for five minutes.

When the blades become dull they should be replaced so they do not break, shred, or crack the nails. You may also opt to purchase an electric toenail filer to round off and smooth the nails after trimming. Be sure to praise Lily for her cooperation. Without it, nail trimming is virtually impossible!

Exercise

Exercise is an important part of Lily's physical and mental health. Lhasa Apsos are busy, active dogs. They enjoy playing games and taking walks just as much as they enjoy a snooze on your lap. It's up to you to develop a healthy exercise program suitable for your companion's age, stage of development, health, and physical abilities.

When you begin to plan Lily's exercise program, remember that she first needs to build up endurance gradually. This requires a regular routine that, over time, may increase in length or vigor. Whatever you do, do not take Lily out for infrequent, strenuous exercise. Start with a moderate exercise program and build it up gradually to a level suitable for her age and health condition. A regular exercise program will improve Lily's cardiovascular endurance and function, build strong bones and joints, and develop muscles and muscle tone. Before you start an exercise program, have her examined by your veterinarian and ask for exercise activity recommendations tailored to her needs and abilities.

Walking or Jogging

Walking or jogging is a great form of exercise. It is also strenuous, so start with short walks each day and gradually increase the distance or speed. Lily's natural pace is different from your own—it is a very fast one! Keep in mind that her small size makes it necessary for her to take several steps to keep up with each of your own. Try to exercise on a soft surface, such as a lawn or the beach. Sidewalks and asphalt are hot, uncomfortable, and hard on the joints upon impact. Rocky or gravel surfaces are also hard on the feet. Be sure to keep long hair trimmed from between Lily's footpads and to check her feet for stickers, torn toenails, cuts, or abrasions at the end of every walk. Treat any sores and discontinue the walks until the lesions have completely healed. If you live in an area with snow, try not to walk Lily on salted roadways and be sure to rinse her feet after each walk so she doesn't develop salt burns. Finally, try to walk on level surfaces, especially if she is young and still in her developmental growth phase, or if she is older, or suffering from arthritis. Climbing hills and

Safe Toys Are the Best

The best toys are those that cannot break or shred, are too big to be swallowed, and also provide dental prophylaxis (gum stimulation and removal of tartar buildup on the teeth).

---

stairs can be very hard on growing bones and joints, or aged hips and joints. Luckily for Lily, she is small and light enough so that if you have to climb hills and stairs, you can carry her.

Swimming

Swimming is one of the best forms of exercise for dogs and humans. It builds stamina and works most of the muscles in the body. Swimming is particularly good for older animals because it allows for exercise without impact or trauma to aged joints and bones. Never leave Lily in the water alone. If she swims in a pool, be certain she knows where the stairs are and train her how to get out of the pool. Also be

sure that she does not become chilled. Rinse out any saltwater or chlorine from her hair and dry her thoroughly after each swim.

Fetch

Lhasa Apsos love to play games and many will fetch and retrieve, although often Lhasas decide to keep the toy and hide it, rather than return it! Any safe toy works well for games, including balls and small dumbbells.

Toys

Lhasa Apsos love interesting toys and they can be very possessive of a favorite toy, carrying it around and hiding it away in a secret place. Lhasas also like to chew on their toys, so whatever toy you buy your pet, assume it will end up being a chew toy, whether it was designed for that purpose or not. With this in mind, always be sure the toys you buy are durable, safe, and do not present a choking hazard.

Chew Toys

Chew toys can enrich Lily's life by providing stimulation of the gums and exercise of the jaws. Some chew toys help reduce tartar

Dangerous Toys

Dangerous Toys	Risks
Rawhide formed into bone shapes	"Knots" or other shapes can obstruct the trachea
Latex toys, rubber toys, cotton ropes, hard plastic toys	May shred or break and obstruct the gastrointestinal tract
Toys small enough to be swallowed	May obstruct trachea or gastrointestinal tract

There's no such thing as too many toys! Just be sure they are safe for your pet!

buildup on the teeth. Chew toys are useful tools to help keep Lily from chewing on valuables, such as furniture or clothing. Never give her an old shoe or piece of clothing as a chew toy. She will not know the difference between an old, discarded item and your most expensive clothing or shoes. By allowing Lily to chew on old shoes, you send the message that anything in your closet is fair game. Don't confuse her!

Not all toys are suitable for Lhasa Apsos. For example, cow hooves, available as chew toys in local pet stores, are very hard and may actually cause a tooth to fracture. Other toys may break, shred, or tear and become lodged in the air passages or gastrointestinal tract.

Traveling with Your Lhasa Apso

Planning a vacation? Visiting friends? Lhasa Apsos love to travel and a well-mannered Lhasa Apso makes a wonderful ambassador for the breed. With careful planning and advance preparation, taking your Lhasa on a trip with you can be a lot of fun.

Your Lhasa will enjoy fetching almost any kind of toy!

There are situations, however, in which traveling with your Lhasa is discouraged. For example, a very old, sick, or debilitated dog should not be subjected to the stresses of travel and would do better staying at home. Nervous, high-strung, or aggressive dogs do not make good travelers. And barking dogs are a real nuisance to fellow travelers, especially in hotels or campgrounds.

Here a few guidelines to help ensure the safety and enjoyment of your travels.

1. Make sure Lily is trained to her travel kennel and feels comfortable and secure inside it. This training begins early in life, by using the travel crate daily as a security den and placing food tidbits in it periodically. When it comes time to take a trip, she will feel at home in her travel kennel and will not fret or be stressed.

2. Obtain a health certificate for travel.
- Make sure Lily is in excellent health and able to make the trip.
- Ask your veterinarian to conduct a physical examination and verify that all necessary vaccinations are up-to-date.
- Ask if any special medications for the trip are recommended (for example, medication for the prevention of heartworm in certain states, or medication for car sickness).

3. Make sure you have all the things you might need during the trip, including items in case of illness or emergency.
- Travel kennel
- Collar with identification tag and leash
- Dishes, food, and bottled water
- Medications

Lhasas love to go for walks. Your pet is ready when you are. Just be sure you start out at a reasonable pace and distance, and exercise on a soft surface!

- First aid kit
- Toys and bedding from home
- Grooming supplies
- Clean-up equipment: pooper scooper, plastic bags, paper towels, and carpet cleaner
- Veterinary records and photo identification

  4. Make reservations in advance.
- Check with hotels or campgrounds to be sure pets are permitted.
- Reserve space for a dog with the airlines if air travel is part of your travel plans.

Air Travel

If you are traveling by air and Lily is accustomed to her travel kennel, tranquilizers are seldom necessary, sometimes ineffective, and often discouraged. Unless Lily is very young, and small enough to fit under the seat in front of you in a travel case, she will be assigned a space in the cargo hold. Be sure to make advance reservations, as there are a limited

number of animals that may travel on a given flight, either in the cabin or in the cargo hold. The cargo hold is temperature controlled and pressurized just like the cabin in which you travel. Don't worry about Lily; she probably will sleep better on the plane than you will!

Automobile Travel

If your plans include travel by car, remember that some dogs have a tendency to become carsick. To reduce the likelihood that Lily will become carsick, limit her food and water three hours before travel begins and place her crate where she can see outside the car. Although dogs become carsick from anxiety about travel, tranquilizers are not always effective in preventing it. Another option you may wish to discuss with your veterinarian is the use of an antihistamine (Antivert, meclizine) that has been shown to be effective for some dogs.

Most important: Remember to never leave your Lhasa Apso in a parked car on a warm day, even for a few minutes. The temperature inside a car, with the windows cracked open and parked in the shade, can quickly soar past

120°F (48.9°C) within a few short minutes and your pet can rapidly die of heatstroke.

Children and Lhasa Apsos

The Lhasa Apso's appeal spans all ages. Children are drawn to the Lhasa Apso for its endearing appearance and small size, and a mutual affection quickly develops between them. Lhasa puppies make good, loyal companions for children.

Proper Handling

It is very important for parents to instruct their children about how to properly handle and care for their new dog. Children should learn that their new pet has needs and feelings that must be respected. They also must be taught not to put their faces up close against an animal. It is very tempting to rub a cheek across the soft fur, or even to try to kiss the new dog, but under the wrong circumstances, accidents can happen and a dog can bite. Because small children are short and their heads are large in proportion to their bodies, the majority of all animal bite wounds inflicted on children (regardless of animal species) happen in the area of the face and head.

Adult Supervision

Of course, the amount of unsupervised interaction and the responsibilities given to children depend on their ages. Toddlers and preschool-age children require very close supervision. They need to be taught how not to harm the

Never leave your Lhasa in an unattended car on a warm day, even with the windows partially rolled down! Temperatures can rise in a very short time, causing heatstroke.

When traveling with your Lhasa, a carrier provides security and comfort in unfamiliar surroundings.

puppy inadvertently. Older children can assume some of the primary care, such as feeding, watering, bathing, and taking the dog for a walk. These daily activities need to be monitored closely by an adult to make sure the dog is not being neglected.

Life Lessons

With adult guidance, there is no limit to the things children can learn from a Lhasa Apso. These wonderful dogs provide an excellent opportunity for adults to teach children about pets, the importance of humane care and treatment, and respect for life. They provide a way for children to learn responsibility by participating in the animal's care, and learning the importance of fresh water, good food, a clean home, and a kind heart.

Some children are frightened or uncomfortable around dogs, especially large ones. Because a Lhasa Apso is small and charming, it can make it possible for a child to replace anxiety, fear, or timidity with tenderness and affection. A Lhasa Apso makes a dear, trustworthy friend for a child, serving as a confidant and a subordinate—something children rarely find. For a growing child, these are precious gifts that help develop confidence and character.

Animal Life and Death

The most difficult thing about owning and loving a pet is the knowledge that even with the very best of care, old age or illness, and eventually death, cannot be avoided. Because Lhasa

Apsos have a relatively long life span compared to other kinds of pets, you and your family will have developed a long friendship and a deep attachment to this canine family member over the years. Children are very sensitive to issues of animal life and death, and the death of a family pet may be the first loss a child experiences. When the time comes to say good-bye to a long-time companion, children are as grief-stricken, if not more so, than adults.

It is very important that the child be prepared in advance for the eventual, and inevitable, loss or death of a beloved pet. It is especially important that this preparation be provided in a compassionate manner appropriate for the child's age and level of maturity. The loss of a pet is a very emotional experience for a child, but if handled skillfully, this loss can be turned into a positive learning experience. It provides an opportunity in which you may openly discuss life, love, illness, or death and possibly address additional fears or concerns the child may have. The sadness from the loss of one special Lhasa will be outweighed by the important role it played as a family member helping a child grow, mature, and strengthen in character.

Your Lhasa will spend as much time on your lap as you let it!

If your pet joins you on a family outing or picnic, make sure it has plenty of shade and a safe place to rest. Keep a close watch on your pet and don't let it wander.

Teach the children in your family to handle a Lhasa puppy gently. Let them love the pup, but don't let them hug or squeeze it too hard!

As your puppy grows, so will its personality and you will naturally become more and more attached to it.

Check with your veterinarian to see if your pet will need heartworm preventive medicine on your trip.

Before you travel with your Lhasa, check with your veterinarian to make sure vaccinations are up-to-date. Your pet can contract diseases and parasites at parks and rest stops.

If you want Lotus to look and feel his very best, a regular grooming program is essential. All Lhasas need to be combed, brushed, and bathed routinely to keep their coats healthy, shiny, and free of mats. Grooming is not just for cosmetic purposes. If Lotus's coat becomes matted, its insulating quality will be lost. Mats are good hiding places for parasites, such as fleas, ticks, and mites. Because severe mats cannot be untangled, you will have to cut them out with scissors, and this can make Lotus look uneven and ragged. By regularly brushing and bathing Lotus, you can observe his overall appearance and condition on a routine basis by checking his skin, eyes, ears, teeth, and nails. You can detect signs of problems (irritated, tearing eyes; foul-smelling ears; lumps, parasites, and sores) early, before they become a serious health problem.

Step One—Teaching Your Lhasa Apso to Stand on the Grooming Table.

You will find that grooming your Lhasa is a lot of fun and a very enjoyable activity for both of you—if your companion is trained to stand still on a grooming table and cooperate. A grooming table allows you to work in various positions at a comfortable level, without bending or stooping, and to obtain the best aesthetic results. If Lotus is not accustomed to a grooming table and is not obedient, you will lose control of the grooming session and that can lead to some clumsy—even dangerous—situations.

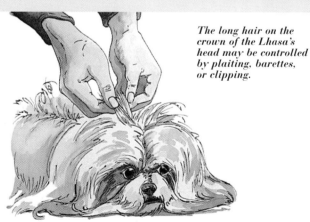

The long hair on the crown of the Lhasa's head may be controlled by plaiting, barettes, or clipping.

Before you can groom Lotus, he must be trained to sit and stand quietly on the table. The key to success is to be gentle and patient, yet firm. Start by placing a rubber nonslip mat on the tabletop and standing Lotus on the mat. Hold him lightly with your hand between his rear legs. If he tries to move or sit down, apply gentle pressure to bring him back to the right position. Don't try to position him by lifting him under the stomach. This will cause him to hunch up. Reassure Lotus by talking to him in a happy voice and petting him. Make this first training session short, no longer than five minutes. When you are finished, praise Lotus for his cooperation, give him a small food reward, and set him on the floor. This is your way of telling him that his time on the table has ended. If desired, you can repeat these mini-training sessions two or three times a day until Lotus feels comfortable and happy standing on the table.

Step Two—Handling, Brushing, and Combing.

Once Lotus is accustomed to standing on the grooming table and remains standing without attempting to jump off the table, you can begin training him to be handled, brushed, and combed. Begin by gently lifting and holding each foot for a few seconds. As he becomes used to having his feet handled, you can hold each foot for longer periods of time and handle each toe individually (as you will have to do later when you trim his nails). Gently handle Lotus's ears, face, body, and tail. When he accepts your handling calmly and remains standing on the table, you can introduce him to a soft brush or a gentle comb. At this point, it really does not matter if you comb out any dirt or tangles. The idea is to let Lotus become accustomed to a strange or unfamiliar object touching his body. Simply place the brush or comb lightly on his back and sides and then begin to gently slide it along the surface of the coat. Don't worry about the face and ears right now. If Lotus seems to enjoy the massage, continue for a few more minutes. Be sure to stop before he tires of it. If you are training a young puppy, remember that puppies bore easily so you may want to limit this session to three to five minutes.

Step Three—Working Around the Face and Toenails.

You may begin working on and around Lotus's face once he has learned to accept having his body brushed and combed. Be sure Lotus is well trained before you work with scissors or other objects near his eyes and ears. Start by scratching the ears, inside and out, and under the chin. Take a soft cotton cloth or tissue and gently wipe the corners of the eyes and then the corners of the nostrils. Lift the lips and open Lotus's mouth. Try to perform these activities in the same order. Make them a brief, but repetitive, routine followed by plenty of praise. Continue to handle and lift the feet. If all is proceeding well, now is a good time to pretend to use the nail clippers. Let Lotus become

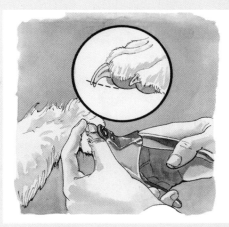

To determine how much nail to trim, imagine a straight line from the bottom of the pad to the toenail. This will help you avoid cutting the quick. The guillotine-type nail trimmer shown here, works well.

familiar with the sound the clippers make, set them on the nails, but do not cut the nails.

Step Four—Detail Work.

It will take several sessions before Lotus has completely adapted to the routine of standing on the grooming table and being handled, brushed, and combed. When you are both ready (and not before!), you can lengthen the sessions and begin to seriously groom his coat. Be careful when you work around Lotus's eyes. To avoid accident or injury, cover his eyes with your hand when you trim stray hairs away with scissors. Pay attention to the feet, trim away excess hair, and keep the toenails at a reasonable length. The grooming table is also a good place to brush Lotus's teeth. You can learn many tricks of the trade from other Lhasa Apso owners or professional dog groomers. The more you practice, the more skilled you will become, and the better Lotus will look!

FEEDING YOUR LHASA APSO

Good nutrition has been recognized for centuries as being one of the most important factors in maintaining health and extending longevity. Of all the countless things you do for your Lhasa Apso, providing a nutritionally complete and balanced diet is one of the most important ways to keep your dog healthy throughout life.

When dogs were first domesticated, their meals consisted of remains from the hunt, vegetables from the garden, and whatever "table scraps" were available. Dogs essentially ate much of the same foods as their owners. Due to the wide variety of foods in their meals, most of the nutritional bases were covered. Commercial dog food was to make its appearance thousands of years later. Dry kibble became popular during World War II, when meat became a scarce commodity. Later, with consumer convenience in mind as people became more pressed for time, and particularly in the past 40 years, we witnessed the evolution of TV dinners, microwave meals, and fast food restaurants. The dog food business was not far behind, ready to capitalize on modern-day lifestyles. It was obvious that families that spent less time cooking for themselves were unlikely to cook for the family dog. Through advertising and excellent marketing strategies,

Excellent nutrition is the best health care you can give your Lhasa.

the convenience of canned or packaged commercial dog food was promoted until it became commonplace. Today, the manufacture and sale of pet food is a multi-billion dollar industry. As with all businesses, profit is a measure of success. This brings us to a key point to keep in mind as we review nutritional choices. Quality nutrition should not cost a fortune, but it certainly is not cheap.

The important role proper nutrition plays in a dog's life cannot be overemphasized. It is the key to overall good health. Fortunately, it is one aspect of Lotus's health care in which you have full control. Don't cut corners when it comes to Lotus's nutrition. Good nutrition will determine his health, development, and life span. With this is mind, let's discuss the kind of nutrition Lotus requires.

Starting Off Right

Before you bring Lotus home, ask the breeder what type of dog food he is currently eating and be sure to obtain at least a two-week supply of the food. Continue feeding the same diet, at least until he has had a chance to adjust to the new family and home. A change in diet during this time of adaptation can be stressful and possibly cause stomach upset or diarrhea. Be sure to take Lotus to your veterinarian within 48 hours of purchase for a physical examination and to plan a complete health care program. The first veterinary visit is an ideal time to discuss specific nutritional requirements and the breeder's recommendations. If a change in diet is appropriate, make the change gradually by increasing the amount of the new diet, and decreasing the amount of the old diet, in small increments at each meal.

Changing Nutritional Needs

Nutritional needs change throughout life, so it makes sense that Lotus's diet also will need to be changed at times. For example, when he is just a puppy, he will need a dog food that provides complete and balanced nutrition for growth and development. As he reaches adolescence, his dietary requirements may lessen or increase, according to his individual needs and activities. When Lotus is an adult, he will have greater nutritional requirements if he is active, doing obedience work, on the show circuit, or being used for breeding purposes, than he would have if he were sedentary. Finally, as Lotus ages, or if he becomes sick or is recovering from an illness, he will need a diet based on his health condition and special needs.

Environment also plays an important role in dietary requirements. If Lotus spends a lot of time outdoors in cold weather, he will have a higher caloric requirement to maintain his normal weight than if he stays indoors in a heated building most of the time.

Finally, genetics can influence a dog's caloric requirements, ability to digest and metabolize certain foods, and ability to maintain a normal weight. If some of Lotus's family members have difficulty maintaining an appropriate weight (if they are overweight or underweight), this may be an inherited tendency and you will have to make a special effort to closely monitor his food source and intake.

For each of Lotus's life stages, you should consult your veterinarian to learn which type of dog food would be most beneficial. The ideal nutrition for him today may not be suitable later in life. With increasing consumer awareness, dog food manufacturers continue to make greater efforts to maintain a competitive edge and offer the dog owner a larger, improved selection of dog foods from which to choose. For these reasons, nutrition will always be an important topic of discussion each time you visit your veterinarian.

Interpreting Dog Food Labels

Today there are countless brands and types of commercial dog foods on the market. Many claim to be the best food you could possibly offer your pet. But how can you be sure? Dog food comes in all sizes, colors, shapes, and consistencies (dry kibble, semi-moist, moist canned). You cannot help but notice how many brands are packaged and named to look and sound more like food for humans than for dogs. This is because the marketing is aimed at you, the consumer. But you are shopping for your dog and he doesn't care what color his food is. He does care how it tastes and smells. Even if you buy a very nutritious dog food, it will not benefit Lotus if he

*The major internal organs
of the Lhasa Apso.*
  1. *nasal sinus*
  2. *larynx*
  3. *trachea*
  4. *lungs*
  5. *heart*
  6. *liver*
  7. *stomach*
  8. *intestine*
  9. *bladder*
  10. *rectum*
  11. *kidneys*
  12. *spleen*
  13. *spinal cord*

refuses to eat it. On the other hand, you don't want to feed an inferior formulation that is not nutritionally balanced simply because he likes the flavor. Sometimes the taste and smell that appeal to a dog are due to food additives, such as artificial flavorings, rather than nutrients.

A good way to select the best dog food for Lotus is to consult with your veterinarian and Lhasa Apso breeders. Another way is to study the dog food labels and select a premium dog food that provides complete and balanced nutrition from high-quality protein sources. But be careful! Dog food labels can be confusing and don't always provide exactly the type of information you want. Here are some definitions to help you decipher and interpret dog food labels.

Ingredients

Ingredients are the materials mixed together to make a specific dog food. Ingredients can be nutritional or non-nutritional substances. Nutritional materials include proteins, fats, carbohydrates, vitamins, and minerals. Non-nutritional substances include food additives, artificial coloring, artificial flavorings, and food preservatives. Dog food labels list ingredients in decreasing order of preponderance by weight. In other words, if the label lists beef, rice, and chicken, this means there is more beef than rice or chicken in the mixture, and more rice than chicken in the mixture. However, it does not mean that there is more beef than rice and chicken combined.

The list of ingredients does not tell you anything about their quality or digestibility. Different dog food manufacturers may use the same types of ingredients, but vary in the quality level. For example, if two different dog foods list chicken as the main ingredient, this doesn't mean the quality of chicken is the same in both

Your Lhasa will look forward to mealtime. Feeding the right amount is as important as feeding the right kind of food. Do not overfeed your pet!

brands. It is important to know which brand contains the most nutritious and easily digested parts of chicken. Unfortunately, that information is not always obvious. For this reason, you cannot rely solely on the comparison of ingredients labels to select dog food.

Nutrients

Nutrients are substances necessary for life. Some nutrients produce energy and some do not. Sugars, amino acids (the building blocks of proteins), and fatty acids are energy-producing nutrients. Water, oxygen, vitamins, and minerals are considered non–energy-producing nutrients. The type and amount of nutrients contained in a dog food mixture is called the nutrient profile.

Nutritional Adequacy

We already have seen that some dog foods are better than others and that good nutrition is not cheap. So it is not surprising to learn that not all dog foods provide adequate nutrition for all dogs. The American Association of Feed Control Officials (AAFCO) requires dog food companies to demonstrate the nutritional adequacy of their products, either by feeding trials or by meeting the AAFCO Nutrient Profile. Feeding trials are the preferred method, but most companies simply calculate a formulation for a diet using a standard table of ingredients. Dog food companies are required to make a statement about the nutritional adequacy of all their products (except treats and snacks), such as "complete and balanced nutrition."

Lhasas can be clever beggars! Don't let your pet connive you into feeding more than its daily ration and don't let it beg at the table!

If you have more than one Lhasa, feed each out of a separate dish so you will know how much each eats. If one of your dogs is a glutton and hogs the food bowls, you will have to feed them in separate areas.

Proteins

Certainly the most important health factor in a dog's diet is protein quality. Protein may come from plant or animal sources; however, not all proteins are created equally. As a general rule, high-quality animal-source proteins are better for dogs than plant-source proteins because they provide a better amino acid balance. Do not confuse a high percentage of protein in the diet with high protein quality. There is a big difference.

Animal protein sources found in commercial dog foods include beef, chicken, turkey, duck, lamb, fish, and eggs. However, just because the protein comes from an animal source does not necessarily indicate it is of high nutritional value. You must read the ingredients label closely and look for words such as "meat," "meal," and "by-products." Meat means muscle and skin, with or without bone. By-products include heads, feet, guts, and bone. By-products are usually less expensive and of poorer quality protein. Meal tells you the protein source has been ground up into particles (as in "cornmeal").

Fats

Fats are important components of your pet's daily diet. They add to the flavor of the food and influence your companion's skin and coat condition. Fats provide energy and play a major role in digestion and the assimilation of fat-soluble vitamins A, D, E, and K. The various fats

(animal fat, vegetable oils, olive oil, fish oils) each have different effects on the body, and many are used for therapeutic remedies.

Carbohydrates

Carbohydrates are sugars, starches, and fibers. They are an inexpensive source of energy compared to high-quality protein. Researchers have not yet determined the exact amount of carbohydrates required in the canine diet, yet carbohydrates make up the major portion of today's commercial dog foods. These carbohydrates usually are provided in the form of corn, corn meal, rice, or a combination of grains. Because dogs cannot digest fiber, it is used in many dog foods to maintain dry matter bulk. Fiber is used extensively in canine weight-reduction diets. Dogs on a high-fiber diet produce a lot more stool volume than dogs on a high-protein diet because much of the food is not digested and is turned into waste matter. If you have several dogs, diet quality becomes an important issue not only in your pets' health, but also in the amount of yard cleanup you have to do.

Vitamins

Good health depends on a balanced vitamin intake in the diet. Depending on how vitamins are absorbed and excreted by the body, they are classified as fat-soluble (vitamins A, D, E, and K) or water-soluble (all the B vitamins and vitamin C). Dogs are capable of making their own vitamin C and do not require supplementation in their diet (unlike humans, nonhuman primates, and guinea pigs, who develop scurvy and die without dietary vitamin C).

Vitamins must be correctly balanced in a dog's diet. Excess vitamin intake, or a vitamin deficiency, can cause serious medical problems.

Minerals

Minerals are necessary for life-sustaining activities that take place in the body on a daily basis, as well as skeletal growth and development, and muscle and nerve function. Minerals include calcium, phosphorus, sodium, potassium, magnesium, zinc, selenium, iron, manganese, copper, iodine, and other chemical elements.

Lhasas, like most dogs, love to eat. By feeding a high-quality dog food, you don't have to sacrifice flavor and palatability for good nutrition.

Like vitamins, minerals should be provided in a balanced ratio. Excessive supplementation of minerals can lead to serious medical conditions.

Additives and Preservatives

Additives and preservatives are substances added to the dog food to improve or enhance color, flavor, and texture, and to extend product shelf life. Additives, such as antioxidants, are added to dog food to help keep fat in the food from becoming rancid over time. Other additives are used to slow down bacterial and fungal growth.

Supplements

If you feed Lotus a high-quality dog food, nutritional supplementation is most likely unnecessary. In fact, by supplementing him with other products, you may disrupt the nutritional balance you are striving to provide. Consult your veterinarian about any form of supplementation before adding it to Lotus's nutritional program.

How Much to Feed

Nutritional needs vary according to the stage of development, activity level, and environmental conditions. Basic feeding guidelines are provided on the dog food label, but the suggested amount per feeding may be more than Lotus requires. Just as you would not eat the same amount of food as your next-door neighbor, no two dogs are alike in their feeding requirements. Although there are all kinds of calculations you

If you have a baby Lhasa that needs supplemental bottle-feeding, your veterinarian can advise you on how much to feed it and which commercial canine formula to use.

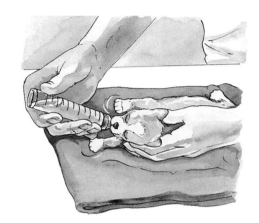

can do to determine Lotus's energy requirements and caloric intake, they probably will vary weekly, and possibly daily, especially if he is a young, active, growing puppy.

The amount you feed Lotus also depends on the quality of the food you provide. If you feed a high-quality dog food that is easily digested, a smaller amount is needed than if you feed a mediocre diet filled with bulk and material (such as fiber) that cannot be digested. You will also notice that Lotus will produce less fecal material when fed a quality diet, because most of the food is used for energy and less is going to waste.

The best way to know if Lotus is eating the proper amount is to check his overall physical condition. You should be able to feel the ribs, but not see them. Weigh him once a week, if possible, and not less than once a month. You can do this by holding Lotus and weighing both of you on a bathroom scale, then weighing yourself alone. Subtract your weight from the combined weight and the difference is Lotus's weight. Another option is to ask your veterinarian if you can use the hospital walk-on platform scale each week. If you notice any weight loss or gain, your veterinarian can advise you if Lotus is within the appropriate weight range and whether to change the diet or meal size. Remember that an adult Lhasa Apso weighs 13 to 15 pounds (6 to 7 kg) and should not exceed 18 pounds (8 kg), so don't let Lotus become too heavy.

When to Feed

Lhasa Apso puppies are active individuals that burn off calories quickly. Their initial growth phase is during the first six months of life, although technically they are still puppies until 8 to 12 months of age, or when they reach puberty. While Lotus is a puppy, he should be fed at least four times a day because he has a small stomach and a high metabolism. As a general guideline, when his growth and development begin to slow down, you can decrease the feeding schedule to three meals (at about 12 weeks of age), and later two meals (at about 6 months of age) a day. Be sure to consult your

TIP

Food Dishes

Use stainless steel food dishes. Plastic or hard rubber dishes can cause skin allergies (contact dermatitis) in some animals.

Lhasas can be finicky eaters and refuse dog food if fed too many table scraps.

Bright eyes and a healthy coat are signs of good nutrition.

All that hair can hide your pet's true shape from you. You should be able to feel its ribs, but they should not protrude and your dog should not feel bony. Feel through the coat to make sure your Lhasa is not too heavy or not too thin.

On warm days your dog will need more water than usual. Make sure fresh water is available at all times.

Your Lhasa's long hair can get wet when it drinks from a bowl. By learning to drink from a water bottle sipper tube, or an automatic waterer (Lix-it), it can keep its ears dry.

Some animals develop skin allergies to plastic or rubber dishes. Using a stainless steel bowl or a heavy lead-free crock will prevent this problem.

Your dog's dietary needs will change throughout its lifetime. A puppy has different nutritional requirements than an adult or senior dog.

veterinarian to be certain this feeding schedule matches Lotus's specific needs.

Unless Lotus is a very active dog, he probably will not require more than one to two meals a day when he is an adult. Ideally the meals should be provided at 12-hour intervals, or if only one meal is provided, in the early evening, after he has exercised and before bedtime. If all of the food has not been eaten after 20 minutes, remove it. An after-dinner leisurely stroll before bedtime will help Lotus sleep more comfortably.

Free Feeding

Some people prefer to feed free choice (also called free feed or *ad libitum*), which means that food is available at all times and the dog eats whenever it desires. This method works well for dogs that are nibblers, not gluttons. Although free choice feeding is convenient, it is difficult to know exactly how much food is eaten daily. It also is not usually successful because most dogs will eat even if they are not hungry. These gourmands eventually will exceed their ideal weight if food is not limited.

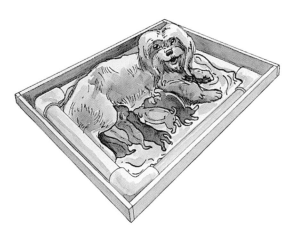

Obesity

Obesity is a form of malnutrition in which there is a ratio of too much fat to lean body tissue. We usually think of malnutrition as being a shortage of food, resulting in a thin, starving individual. However, malnutrition means bad nutrition (from the French word "mal" for "bad"). Malnutrition refers to all aspects of unbalanced nutrition, whether it is too little or too much.

Obesity in dogs has now reached epidemic proportions in the United States—more than 30 percent of the canine population is obese. Overfeeding (especially overfeeding a puppy or adolescent) and inactivity can cause obesity, which in turn can lead to heart disease, skeletal and joint problems (such as arthritis), and metabolic diseases (such as diabetes).

Water

Water is the most important of all nutrients. Water is necessary for life because it is needed for digestion, to metabolize energy, and to eliminate waste products from the body. Although you would never deprive Lotus of food, he could survive longer without food than without water. A 10 percent body water loss will result in death, and water makes up more than 70 percent of your companion's lean adult body weight.

Dogs lose body water throughout the day, in the urine and feces, by evaporation, panting, drooling, and footpad sweating. Water depletion occurs more rapidly in warm or hot weather or when an animal is active. Body water must be replaced continually, so it is extremely important

A Lhasa that is pregnant or nursing has special additional nutritional needs.

that fresh water be available at all times to avoid dehydration and illness.

It is important to monitor how much water Lotus drinks each day. If he seems to be continually thirsty or to drink more than usual, it could be a warning sign for possible illness, such as diabetes or kidney disease. If he is not drinking as much as he should, he can become dehydrated and develop a medical condition. Adequate water intake is especially important in older animals, because they may have impaired kidney function. If you think Lotus is drinking too much, or not drinking enough, contact your veterinarian right away.

Food Myths

There are some common food myths about the effects of various foods in the canine diet. Garlic is often credited with killing worms and repelling fleas. Brewer's yeast and onions also have been touted as flea repellants. Unfortunately, these foods have no action against internal or external parasites, although dogs can benefit from the B vitamins in Brewer's yeast. Onions, on the other hand, can cause toxicity in dogs and are not recommended in the diet.

Food Allergies

Just like people, dogs can develop allergies to certain foods. For example, some dogs are sensitive to corn (a major ingredient in many commercial dog foods) or corn oil, or beef in the diet.

Food allergies often express themselves by their effect on the animal's skin and coat. If Lotus is scratching his skin excessively, for no apparent reason, and his coat does not look its best, ask your veterinarian if a change to a hypoallergenic diet would be beneficial.

Developing Good Eating Habits

✔ Designate a place for the dog food bowl and put everything Lotus is to eat in the bowl. This will discourage him from begging food from your hands or from the dinner table.

✔ Feed on a regular schedule.

✔ Do not feed Lotus human snack foods and candies. They are high in sugars and salts.

✔ Do not feed meat, fish, poultry, or eggs raw. These products can be contaminated with *Salmonella*, *E. coli*, or other bacterial pathogens that can cause fatal illness.

✔ Do not feed bones. They can splinter and become lodged in the throat or gastrointestinal tract.

✔ Determine in advance which food treats, and how many, Lotus will be allowed each day. Do not exceed the limit you have set.

✔ Feed snacks and treats primarily as training rewards or special praise.

✔ Teach children not to feed meals or give treats to Lotus without your permission.

✔ Do not allow Lotus in the kitchen while you are preparing food, or in the dining room during family mealtime. This prevents begging.

KEEPING YOUR LHASA APSO HEALTHY

It's hard to believe that not so long ago we had no way to prevent or treat most canine health problems. It was common for dogs to die from a wide variety of health problems, including malnutrition, severe parasitism, and bacterial and viral diseases. Today's Lhasa Apso is a lucky dog indeed, benefiting from all the medical advances, prescription products, good nutrition, and creature comforts that people enjoy.

Veterinarians today have received many years of training in medicine and surgery and many veterinary clinics are subject to inspection and accreditation. If Lily requires medical expertise in a specific area, board certified veterinary specialists are available to help.

It is reassuring to know so many resources are available if they are ever needed, but the best way to keep your pet healthy is to avoid or prevent problems before they start. Preventive health care is the most important care you can give your dog. It includes regular physical examinations, vaccinations against disease, an effective parasite control program, correct nutrition (see Feeding Your Lhasa Apso), regular exercise, good dental care, routine grooming

Your Lhasa depends on you for everything, including good health care.

(see At Home with Your Lhasa Apso), and plenty of love and attention for her physical and emotional well-being.

Selecting a Veterinarian

You and your veterinarian will be partners sharing responsibility for ensuring your companion's health throughout her life. For this reason, you should be as particular about choosing Lily's veterinarian as you are about your own doctor. Fortunately, there is no shortage of excellent veterinarians, but how do you find the veterinarian that's just right for you and Lily? Here are some guidelines to help you in the selection process.

1. Ideally, you should try to find a veterinarian who appreciates Lhasa Apsos as much as you do and who is familiar with the breed's

An eye examination tells a lot about your pet's health and should be a part of every routine physical examination.

special characteristics. Start looking for a veterinarian before you need one.

2. Ask satisfied Lhasa Apso owners and members of the local kennel clubs which veterinarians they recommend in your area. Word of mouth is one of the best ways to find a veterinarian. Many veterinarians advertise in telephone directories, but the size or style of an advertisement is not an indicator of the best match for your requirements.

3. Consider convenience. What are the doctors' office hours, schedule, and availability? Who is available on weekends and holidays, or in case of emergency? How close is the veterinary clinic or hospital? Will you be able to travel there within a reasonable amount of time in the event of an emergency?

4. Is there a consistency of personnel and continuity of communication? The veterinary support staff will play an important role in Lily's health care. Have the veterinary technicians (animal health care nurses) received formal, certified training, and are they licensed?

5. What are the fees for services? Most veterinarians provide a price estimate for anticipated services and expect payment when service is rendered. Be sure to ask what types of payment methods are available.

6. Request an appointment to tour the veterinary hospital facilities. Examine all of the hospital during your tour, particularly its cleanliness and odors, the surgical suites and isolation wards, and the availability of monitoring equipment for surgery and anesthesia.

You and your veterinarian will develop a relationship of mutual respect and trust. You will rely on each other for accurate information and work together as a team. The chemistry among you, your veterinarian, and Lily should be just right.

Preventive Health Care

Physical Examinations

You know your companion better than anyone. You know when Lily is happy and feeling great, and you will be the first to notice if she is not acting like herself, seems depressed, doesn't want to eat, is limping, is losing weight, or has any other problems. Of course, under these circumstances you would call your veterinarian to schedule an appointment for a physical examination, diagnosis, and treatment. However, the more you know about Lily's condition, and the sooner you recognize any potential problems, the more you can help her—and your veterinarian.

Home Examinations

A home physical examination is a good way to detect a possible problem before it becomes serious. The home examination is not a replacement for the veterinary examination, but it gives you a good idea of your dog's health condition. If you notice something wrong with Lily, call your veterinarian right away and describe your observations and concerns. Keep a record of Lily's condition, noting the date and the time. Add information to the record if there are any changes. This information will be useful in assessing the progression or improvement of a condition over time.

To detect illness in an animal, you must first be able to recognize normal appearance, attitude, stance, movement, and behavior. Here are a few things to look for when you examine your Lhasa Apso.

1. First, watch Lily from a distance. Does she have a happy attitude and does she appear to be in good condition? Is her coat healthy? Does she appear contented and playful? Is she well proportioned (not too thin, not too heavy)? Do you see anything unusual?

2. Observe Lily while she stands. Does she stand naturally and place her weight on all four feet, or is she favoring one foot? If her back is hunched up she may have back or abdominal pain. A drooping head may mean neck pain. A tilted head could indicate ear pain, ear infection, parasites in the ear, or a nervous system problem.

3. Now watch Lily's movement and gaits. Does she walk, trot, and run willingly and normally, or does she move with difficulty, or limp?

An otoscope aids the veterinarian in examining deep inside the ear canal.

TIP

Taking Your Lhasa's Temperature

Normal body temperature for a Lhasa Apso ranges from 99.5 to 102.5°F (37.5 to 39°C). An excited dog may have an elevated temperature as high as 103.5°F (39.3°C), but it should not exceed this value. Lubricate the tip of the thermometer with Vaseline or Aquaphor and gently insert it approximately two inches into the rectum. Wait two minutes, or if you are using a digital thermometer, wait for the beep, then check the temperature reading.

This might be hard to determine because Lhasa Apsos move very quickly! Does Lily seem to experience pain when you handle her feet or legs? The origin of lameness is often difficult to detect, especially if the dog is lame in more than one limb. Lameness could be due to injury,

joint problems, muscular or skeletal problems, or nervous system problems. Often, lameness is due to a foreign object, like a thorn in the footpad, or a grass awn lodged between the toes, so be sure to check all four of Lily's feet.

4. Now look at Lily up close, from the nose to the toes. And yes, a cold, wet nose is normal for a dog, although a dry nose does not necessarily mean she is sick. The nose should be free of discharge (thick mucus or pus), but it is not unusual for dirt to lodge in the little "corner grooves" of her nose (the nares). This can be cleaned away gently with a soft tissue or cotton-tipped swab and warm water. If the nares become sore or raw, you can spread a thin layer of Vaseline or Aquaphor over the area, taking care not to plug the nasal passages. Frequent applications are usually necessary because dogs will lick off medication on the nose shortly after it is applied.

5. Check Lily's eyes. They should be bright and clear. If any mucus has accumulated

Your Lhasa's emotional well-being plays a major role in its physical health.

around the eyes, gently remove it with a tissue. With blunt scissors you may want to trim some of the hair around the eyes to prevent irritation and excessive tearing. Consult your veterinarian if you notice any discharge from the eyes, squinting, redness of the eyes or eyelids, or if the colored part of the eye (the iris) appears hazy or cloudy. Corneal injuries can be very painful, especially in bright light, and require immediate veterinary attention.

6. Look inside Lily's mouth. Are the gums bright pink? Are the teeth free of tartar accumulation, or do they need to be cleaned and polished? Does Lily have bad breath? It has been estimated that more than 85 percent of adult dogs suffer from some degree of periodontal disease and this can cause bad breath. Depending on the odor, some types of bad breath can also indicate a metabolic problem, such as ketosis.

7. Look inside Lily's ears. Lhasas frequently need to have the hair plucked or trimmed from the inside of their ears to prevent the ear canal from becoming moist, thickened, and matted with wax. If Lily's ears are overly sensitive, red, or have a foul odor, contact your veterinarian immediately for medical treatment. If she shakes her head or scratches at her ears, it could mean she has an ear infection or parasites, such as ear mites.

8. Now look at Lily's hair and skin. Is the skin healthy, or is it dry and flaky, or greasy? Is there evidence of parasitism, such as fleas or ticks?

9. Take your pet's pulse. You can do this by simply pressing your fingers against the inside middle portion of her upper thigh. Normal heart rate will range between 80 and 120 beats per minute, depending on whether she is at rest or has just been very active.

10. If Lily has not been spayed, check her regularly for signs of estrus. You don't want to leave her within reach of unwanted suitors during her estrous cycle. If you have an intact male (not neutered), both of his testicles should be fully descended into the scrotum. If one or both testicles are missing, give your veterinarian a call. Retained testicles may be an inherited problem. If the retained testicle is not surgically removed, it can become cancerous in later life. Finally, check under the tail for signs of problems such as swelling, hernias, anal gland problems, cysts, inflammation, diarrhea, and parasites (tapeworms).

Vaccinations

Vaccinations are the best method currently available to protect Lily against serious, life-threatening diseases. Although you will do your best to prevent her from coming into contact with sick animals, at some time your companion will be exposed to disease organisms,

Vaccination Schedule for Puppies

Vaccine	Age for 1st Inoculation	Age for 2nd Inoculation	Age for 3rd Inoculation
Distemper	8 weeks	12 weeks	16 weeks
Hepatitis	8 weeks	12 weeks	16 weeks
Parvovirus	8 weeks	12 weeks	16 weeks*
Parainfluenza	8 weeks	12 weeks	16 weeks
Leptospirosis	12 weeks	16 weeks	
Bordetella	12 weeks	16 weeks	
Lyme Disease**	12 weeks	16 weeks	
Coronavirus***	8 weeks	12 weeks	
Rabies****	12 weeks	15 months	

*Some veterinarians recommend a 4th parvovirus vaccination at 20 weeks of age because some animals do not develop sufficient immunity against this disease before 5 months of age.
**Check with your veterinarian to see if Lyme Disease is a problem in your area or in any areas in which you will be traveling with your pet.
***Coronavirus vaccination may not be necessary. Consult your veterinarian.
****Rabies vaccination intervals vary according to state laws and the type of vaccines used. Consult your veterinarian.

Note: Adult booster vaccinations should be given as recommended by your veterinarian based on your dog's health and specific requirements.

Common Canine Diseases

Disease	Cause	Spread	Contagion
Distemper	Viral	Airborne, body excretions	Highly contagious, especially among young dogs
Parvovirus	Viral	Contaminated feces	Highly contagious, especially among puppies
Infectious Canine Hepatitis	Viral	Body excretions, urine	Highly contagious, especially among puppies and young dogs
Leptospirosis	Bacterial	Urine contaminated in kennels or from wild animals	Highly contagious
Parainfluenza Bordetellosis Both cause "kennel cough"	Viral Bacterial	Airborne, sneeze and cough droplets	Highly contagious, especially in boarding kennels and dog shows
Coronavirus	Viral	Feces	Highly contagious
Lyme Disease	Bacterial	Spread by the bite of an infected tick or contaminated body fluids	
Rabies	Viral	Saliva (bite wounds)	

whether you know it or not. Anywhere you take her—parks, rest stops, campgrounds, dog shows, obedience classes, or even your veterinarian's office—Lily might be exposed to germs that could cause severe illness and possibly death. Although there is not a vaccine available for every known canine disease, we do have vaccines for the most common and deadly diseases.

No vaccine is 100 percent guaranteed effective; however, if you are conscientious about Lily's health and vaccination schedule, you can rest assured she has a very good chance of being protected against serious illness.

You may note that veterinarians may recommend different vaccination schedules. This is because vaccinations should be a medical deci-

Symptoms	Treatment
Respiratory: difficulty breathing, coughing, discharge from nose and eyes. Gastrointestinal: vomiting, diarrhea, dehydration. Nervous: trembling, blindness, paralysis, seizures. Skin: pustules on skin, hard footpads.	None. Supportive therapy only
Gastrointestinal: diarrhea, dehydration, vomiting. Cardiac: heart problems and heart failure.	None. Supportive therapy only
Liver: inflammation, jaundice. Eyes: "blue eye" due to inflammation and fluid buildup. Kidney: damage. Pain and internal bleeding.	None. Supportive therapy only
Kidney: damage and failure. Liver: damage and jaundice. Internal bleeding, anemia.	Antibiotics
Respiratory: dry, hacking, continual cough of several weeks duration that may cause permanent damage to airways	Supportive therapy including antibiotics
Gastrointestinal symptoms: vomiting, diarrhea, dehydration	None. Supportive therapy only
Swollen lymph nodes, lethargy, loss of appetite, joint swelling, lameness, can induce heart and kidney disease	Supportive therapy including antibiotics
Fatal, preceded by nervous system signs including paralysis, incoordination, and change in behavior	None (post-exposure treatment does exist for humans)

sion, not a calendar event. In other words, the type of vaccination and when it is administered should be appropriate to your Lhasa Apso's lifestyle, age, health condition, past medical history, and potential risk of exposure. Another reason vaccine schedules may vary is that most vaccine label recommendations are based on historical precedent. For example, it has been found that by vaccinating large populations of animals annually there has been a decline in disease incidence in the overall canine population. However, it has not yet been scientifically demonstrated that vaccinations must be given every year. In fact, vaccines vary in range of purity, potency, safety, and efficacy. Vaccination is a potent medical procedure with profound

Protect your pet from harsh weather and don't let it get chilled. Be sure to bring your pet inside and dry it off well after it has played in the rain or snow.

Puppies can get themselves into trouble! Make sure your puppy can't climb up on things, slip off objects, or fall out of a window!

Lhasas are very well behaved and make excellent house dogs.

Vaccination is a medical decision, not a calendar event. Consult your veterinarian for the vaccine schedule appropriate for your dog's needs.

Be sure to check your pet's feet after every outing. You may have to remove foreign objects (thorns, burrs, grass awns) from between your pet's toes.

Lhasas are hardy little dogs. With good care they can live 15 years or more.

Never buy a puppy as a gift for someone, especially during the holidays.

Common Parasitic Conditions

Internal Parasites	Mode of Transmission to Dogs
Roundworms	Ingestion of eggs in feces of infected animals, transmitted from mother to pup in utero or in the milk
Hookworms	Ingestion of larvae in feces of infected animals, direct skin contact with larvae
Whipworms	Contact with feces
Tapeworms	Contact with fleas and feces, ingestion of fleas, eating raw meat (wild rodents)
Heartworms	Mosquito bite
Protozoa	Contact with feces

External Parasites	Animal Health Problem
Fleas	Allergy to flea saliva, skin irritation and itching, transmission of tapeworms
Ticks	Transmission of Lyme Disease, skin irritation and infection
Sarcoptic mange	Skin lesions and itching, hair loss
Demodectic mange	Skin lesions, localized or generalized hair loss

impact. There are significant benefits, as well as some risks, associated with any vaccine. Vaccine administration should always take into consideration the animal's risk of exposure (population density), susceptibility or resistance to disease, and overall health (nutrition, parasites, age, special medical conditions).

For these reasons, the following vaccination schedule should be considered only as a guideline. Your veterinarian will determine Lily's indi-vidual vaccination program depending on her needs and health at the time of examination.

Parasite Control

Giant strides have been made in recent year regarding parasite control, both internal (roundworms, hookworms, whipworms, tapeworms, and heartworms) and external (fleas, ticks, and mange-causing mites). Many products of the past have been replaced by recent,

Mode of Transmission to Humans	Prevention
Accidental ingestion of eggs from contact with infected fecal material	Parasiticides should be administered to pups as early as 3 weeks of age and should be repeated regularly as necessary
Direct skin contact with larvae in soil contaminated with feces of infected animals, accidental ingestion of larvae	Parasiticides
None	Parasiticides
Accidental ingestion of larvae	Parasiticides
None	Parasiticides
Accidental ingestion of organisms	Parasiticides

Contagious to Humans

Fleas may bite humans. Tapeworms also may be indirectly transmitted to people.

Humans can contract Lyme Disease from direct contact with ticks. Always wear gloves when removing ticks from your dog, to avoid contracting the disease.

Sarcoptic mange can spread from pets to people by contact.

None

convenient parasiticides. For example, prevention and treatment of internal parasites, heartworm prevention, and treatment for flea infestation can all be accomplished by giving your dog a single tablet monthly. There is a variety of pharmaceuticals available to prevent and treat internal and external parasites on a once-a-month basis. These effective, new products are available only from your veterinarian and require a physical examination, a heart-

worm test, and fecal examination, prior to dispensing.

Internal parasites: Internal parasites (such as worms and protozoa) can have a serious impact on a dog's health. They can cause diarrhea, and in severe cases dehydration and malnutrition. In addition, many internal parasites of dogs are transmitted through contact with feces and can pose a serious health threat to people, especially children. This is why it is important to keep Lily in a clean environment and to teach children to wash their hands before eating or after handling any dog.

Illness

If you have to ask yourself whether you should call your veterinarian, then it's a safe bet that you should. If Lily was looking and acting completely healthy and normal, you wouldn't be asking yourself that question. Better to be safe and contact your veterinarian if you think your pet is having a problem. Treating the condition at its very onset can make all the difference between rapid recovery and prolonged illness.

After conducting a physical examination on your companion, contact your veterinarian to discuss any abnormal or unusual findings.

Some abnormal findings may not suggest an illness in and of themselves (such as loss of appetite or listlessness), but they are good indicators that Lily is experiencing other medical problems that require veterinary attention. Contact your veterinarian if Lily is having any of the following problems:

- ✔ Fever
- ✔ Pain
- ✔ Loss of appetite
- ✔ Lethargy
- ✔ Vomiting
- ✔ Diarrhea
- ✔ Coughing
- ✔ Sneezing
- ✔ Wheezing
- ✔ Difficulty breathing
- ✔ Difficulty swallowing
- ✔ Choking
- ✔ Limping
- ✔ Head shaking
- ✔ Trembling
- ✔ Blood in the urine or stools
- ✔ Inability to urinate
- ✔ Inability to have a bowel movement
- ✔ Severe constipation
- ✔ Dehydration
- ✔ Weight loss

First Aid for Your Lhasa Apso

In spite of all your efforts to provide a safe environment for your Lhasa Apso, accidents can happen and many are life-threatening. The difference between life and death may depend on how prepared you are in an emergency situation. Be sure to have all your supplies on hand in advance so you do not waste precious time during an emergency trying to find what you need. As soon as possible, assemble a first aid emergency kit for Lily. Set aside a special place for the kit. Keep your veterinarian's daytime and

It's fun to play outside but watch out for bees, wasps, hornets, and spiders!

Keep your pet indoors on hot days. Never leave your Lhasa outside without shelter from the sun, wind, and rain.

emergency telephone numbers near the phone and keep an additional copy of emergency telephone numbers in the first aid emergency kit.

Supplies for Your Emergency First Aid Kit

There are some basic supplies and materials you need for your emergency first aid kit. These items are available from your veterinarian or local drug store. You will no doubt think of additional things to include in the kit for when you travel or are away from home. For example, bottled water, balanced electrolyte solution (Pedialyte), medication to prevent car-sickness, tranquilizers, and pain killers (available from your veterinarian) are practical items to keep on hand.

Emergency First Aid Care

The goal of first aid treatment is to give Lily whatever emergency care she requires to save her life or reduce pain and suffering until you can contact your veterinarian. Before you begin any first aid treatment, the most important thing to remember is to protect yourself from being bitten or injured. Your usually loving pet may behave unpredictably when it is in pain or frightened. Your pet may not recognize you or may instinctively lash out in self-defense at anyone who approaches it. If someone else is available, you can save time by having the person contact your veterinarian for advice while you begin emergency treatment. You may need assistance restraining Lily while you treat her, so be sure the person you

ask for assistance is experienced in animal handling. Always muzzle your dog before initiating emergency treatment, for the safety of your pet and everyone involved.

Bite wounds: Bite wounds commonly result from battles with other dogs, cats, or wild animals. In addition to thorough cleansing, bite wounds usually require antibiotic therapy to prevent infection. If the wound is a tear, it may need to be sutured. If the injury is a puncture wound, it should be cleaned well with hydrogen peroxide and allowed to remain open and drain. Be sure to consult your veterinarian immediately regarding any bite wound injuries. Antibiotics may be necessary to prevent bacterial infection. In the unlikely event that a stray animal or a wild animal (raccoon, skunk, bat) has bitten Lily, you need to discuss the possible risk of rabies with your veterinarian.

Bleeding: Bleeding can occur from injury, trauma, or serious health problems. The first thing you should do is apply firm pressure over the wound to stop the bleeding. If you do not have a gauze or clean towel, any readily available, clean, absorbent material can be used as a compress. If a large blood vessel in a limb has

Emergency First Aid Kit

Item	Purpose
Hydrogen peroxide 3 percent	Clean cuts and wounds, induce vomiting
Povidone iodine solution	Clean and disinfect wounds
Triple antibiotic ointment	Topical application to cuts and wounds
Kaopectate	Treat diarrhea
Milk of magnesia	Treat constipation
Ipecac syrup	Induce vomiting
Saline solution (sterile)	Flush and rinse wounds, can be used as an eyewash

Additional supplies:
1. Bandage scissors
2. Small, regular scissors
3. Thermometer
4. Tourniquet (an old necktie will work)
5. Tweezers
6. Forceps
7. Mouth gag
8. Cotton balls
9. Q-tips
10. Roll of gauze bandage
11. Gauze pads (such as Telfa no-stick pads)
12. Elastic bandage (preferably waterproof)
13. Activated charcoal (in case of poisoning)
14. Muzzle (an old necktie will work)
15. Blanket (to provide warmth or to use as a stretcher)
16. Paper towels
17. Exam gloves (vinyl is preferable to latex because some people are allergic to latex)
18. Flashlight

been severed, it may be necessary to apply a tourniquet above the cut area. Be sure to loosen the tourniquet every 15 minutes to relieve pressure and allow circulation. Contact your veterinarian.

Bone fractures: Signs of bone fractures include swelling, pain and tenderness, abnormal limb position or movement, limping, and crepitation (crackling sensation when the area is touched). When bones are broken, they may remain under the skin or protrude up through the skin (open fracture).

If Lily breaks a leg, and the bone is not exposed, you can make a temporary splint out of a small, flat piece of wood. First, muzzle your Lhasa Apso, then gently tape the splint to the leg, allowing an overlap at each end of the break site. Do not wrap the splint to the leg so tightly that the paw swells and do not wrap tape around the injury. If the bone is exposed, do not try to replace it or cleanse it. Stop the bleeding and cover the wound with a sterile bandage. Make sure Lily does not contaminate the open fracture by licking it. Contact your veterinarian immediately for advice. Lily should receive veterinary care for the broken bone(s) as soon as possible, and definitely within 24 hours.

Burns: Your Lhasa Apso can suffer three kinds of burns:

✔ Thermal burns—fire, boiling liquids, appliances

✔ Electrical burns—chewing on electrical cords

✔ Chemical burns—a variety of chemicals (such as corrosives, oxidizing agents, desiccants, and poisons)

If Lily is burned, immediately cool the burn by applying a cold, wet cloth or an ice pack to the area. Protect the burned area from the air with an ointment (Neosporin or *Aloe vera*). If she has suffered a chemical burn, immediately flush the burn profusely with water or saline to dilute and rinse the caustic chemical from the area. Do not allow Lily to lick the area or she will burn her mouth and esophagus with the substance. Contact your veterinarian immediately.

Choking occurs when an object (bones, food, toys, rocks) becomes trapped, or lodged, in the mouth or throat. In this case, your pet is in immediate danger of accidentally inhaling the foreign object. If the object obstructs the air

TIP

Muzzles

If you have not yet purchased a muzzle from the pet store, you can make a muzzle using an old necktie, rolled gauze, or a cloth strip about 18 inches (45 cm) long and 2 inches (5 cm) wide.

Wrap the gauze around the snout and mouth, making sure it does not pull on all the hair around the face, and tie it securely under the chin (this will not affect Lily's ability to breath). Take the ends of the gauze and tie them behind the head, on top of the neck. This muzzle will not hurt your pet and will protect you from being bitten. Make sure Lily does not try to remove the muzzle with her front paws.

In an emergency, a tie can be fashioned into an effective muzzle. It should be tied snugly, but not too tightly.

passageway, Lily will suffocate. If she is choking, you will need a good, clear view of her mouth and throat to see if the offending object can be found and safely removed. Lhasa Apsos have small jaws. It will be difficult to look into her mouth. A short wooden dowel—2-3 inches (5-6 cm) in diameter—inserted between the back molars, may serve as a gag to hold the mouth open while you use a flashlight to take a closer look down the throat. If you see the foreign object, be very careful not to push it further down the throat or into the trachea (windpipe). Remove the object with forceps when possible, to avoid being bitten.

Cuts: Cuts should be cleansed well and treated properly to prevent infection. Sometimes it is difficult to tell how deep the cut is. Serious cuts may require sutures, so be sure to contact your veterinarian for advice. If the cut is not too deep, wash it with a mild soap and rinse it several times with water. Disinfect the injury with hydrogen peroxide or Betadine solution. (Hydrogen peroxide is especially useful for treating puncture wounds.) Dry the wound well and apply an antibiotic ointment to it. If the cut is in an area that can be bandaged, wrap the area with gauze and elastic bandage to prevent contamination and infection. Change the bandage daily.

Dystocia: Dystocia is the term used when a pregnant female has difficulty giving birth to her young. Dystocia occurs when the smooth muscles of the uterus become fatigued and weakened and can no longer contract. Dystocia also occurs when the uterus becomes twisted, or when the mother's pelvic area is abnormal or too small to allow passage of the puppy. In some cases, dystocia occurs because the puppy is too large or not in an appropriate birth position. (It is normal for puppies to be born either hindfeet and rump first or headfirst.)

Dystocia is a medical emergency that requires veterinary expertise. Medications to stimulate uterine contractions, or surgery, may be required to successfully deliver live pups. For this reason, it is a good idea to give your veterinarian advance notice of Lily's delivery due date and make backup arrangements for emergency care if your veterinarian is unavailable the day she gives birth (whelps).

A good rule of thumb is not to allow Lily to be in hard labor for more than two hours. If she has not whelped a pup within that time period, or if she has stopped labor altogether, she needs help. Contact your veterinarian immediately.

Heatstroke: Heatstroke is caused by exposure to high temperature and stress. Confinement in a car is one of the leading causes of heatstroke. On a hot day, a car parked in the shade, with the windows partially open, can still reach temperatures exceeding 120°F (48.9°C) within a few minutes. Overexertion on a hot day can also cause heatstroke. Dogs that are old or overweight are especially prone to heatstroke.

Signs of heatstroke include rapid breathing, panting, bright red gums, vomiting, diarrhea, dehydration, and a rectal temperature of 105 to 110°F (41 to 43°C). As the condition progresses, the body organs become affected, the animal weakens, goes into shock, then a coma, and dies. All of this can happen in a very short period of time and death can occur rapidly.

If Lily is suffering from heatstroke, the first thing you must do is lower her body temperature immediately. You can do this by placing her in a tub filled with cold water. Be sure to keep Lily's head above the water, especially if she is unconscious, so that she does not drown. Do not try to give Lily water to drink if she is unconscious. If a tub is unavailable, you can cool your pet by hosing her with a garden hose or applying ice packs to her body.

Heatstroke is a medical emergency that requires veterinary care. Lily will need to be treated with intravenous fluids and various medications to treat shock and prevent cerebral edema (brain swelling). Contact your veterinarian immediately.

Eye injury: Eye injuries are extremely painful. The sooner you obtain treatment for Lily's eyes, the sooner you can relieve your companion's pain and increase the chances of saving her eyes and vision. Injured eyes are very sensitive to the light and exposure to even subdued lighting can hurt the eyes. If Lily's injury is such that it requires flushing and rinsing the eye, you can do this using a commercial eyewash solution or saline solution intended for use in the eyes. Place Lily in a dark place and contact your veterinarian immediately. When you transport her to the hospital, place her in a travel crate and cover the crate with a blanket to keep out as much light as possible.

Insect stings: If a bee stings Lily, remove the stinger with tweezers (wasps and hornets do not leave their stingers). Try to gently remove the stinger without squeezing the base (where part of the bee's body is attached) so that additional venom is not injected into the site. This can be tricky, as the bee's stinger is barbed and the more you push on it, the deeper it penetrates.

Apply a paste mixture of water and baking soda or an ice pack to the area to relieve pain. You may also put a topical antihistamine cream around the stung area. Watch Lily closely for the next two hours for signs of illness.

Most cases of bee, hornet, and wasp stings are nothing more than painful annoyances.

However, some animals develop a hypersensitivity to insect stings that can lead to anaphylactic shock and death. If the swelling worsens, or if Lily becomes restless and has difficulty breathing, or starts to vomit, develops diarrhea, or loses consciousness, then contact your veterinarian immediately. This is a life-threatening situation and immediate professional treatment is necessary.

Poisoning: In addition to insect venom poisons, pets can be poisoned by eating or inhaling toxic substances, or by contact with poisons on their skin, mucous membranes, or eyes.

Signs of poisoning include restlessness, drooling, abdominal pain, vomiting, diarrhea, unconsciousness, seizures, shock, and death. Common sources of poison include rodent bait, houseplants, insecticides, medication overdose, spoiled food, antifreeze (ethylene glycol), and chocolate. (Chocolate contains theobromine, a substance similar to caffeine that is toxic to dogs.)

If you know the source of Lily's poisoning, contact your veterinarian immediately for advice. If the poison came in a container (for example, antifreeze or rodent poison), read the container label and follow the emergency instructions for treating poisoning. If the instructions state to induce vomiting, you may accomplish this by administering one-half ml per pound of body weight syrup of ipecac, or one-half teaspoon of hydrogen peroxide 3 percent for every 10 pounds of body weight.

Activated charcoal is a good compound to use to dilute and adsorb ingested poisons. You can obtain activated charcoal in powder or tablet form from your veterinarian to keep in your first aid kit. If you do not have activated

Administering medication is an important technique to master. Open the jaws as shown here by placing your thumb and index finger behind the upper canines.

charcoal, and you do not have any products to induce vomiting, you can dilute the poison in the gastrointestinal tract by giving Lily some milk. Do not try to give her any medication if she is unconscious.

The sooner the poisoning is diagnosed and treated, the better Lily's chances of full recovery. Most poisonings require veterinary treatment in addition to the initial emergency care you provide. Contact your veterinarian immediately if you suspect Lily has been exposed to poison.

Seizures: There are many causes of seizures, including epilepsy, poisoning, and brain trauma. Seizures may be mild or severe, ranging from a mild tremor of short duration to violent convulsions, chomping jaws and frothing at the mouth, stiffening of the neck and limbs, and cessation of breathing. During a severe seizure, a dog is not conscious and can be hurt thrashing about on the floor. Lily may seem to be choking during a seizure, but avoid the temptation to handle her mouth, as you will be bitten. If her jaws clamp down on your fingers,

the jaws will not release until the seizure has ended. Simply try to prevent Lily from injuring herself or hitting her head until the seizure has ended. After a seizure, Lily will be exhausted and seem dazed. Place her in a quiet room with subdued light. Keep her comfortable and warm and when she is conscious offer her some water to drink. Contact your veterinarian immediately for follow-up medical care, and to determine the cause of the seizure and how to prevent another one from occurring.

Shock: Shock is a condition in which there is a decreased blood supply to vital organs and the body tissues die from inadequate energy production. Blood loss, heatstroke, bacterial toxins, and severe allergic reactions all can cause an animal to go into shock.

Shock is a serious emergency situation that results in a rapid death unless immediate veterinary care—including fluid and oxygen therapy and a variety of medications—is available. Signs of shock include vomiting, diarrhea, weakness, difficulty breathing, increased heart rate, collapse, and coma.

Snakes, toads, lizards, and spiders: Even a pampered house dog can encounter some danger, whether in the backyard or on a camping trip. Being aware of these potential problems can help you prepare in case of emergency.

Poisonous snakebites. There are three groups of venomous snakes in North America: the pit vipers, which include the rattlesnake, copperhead, and water moccasin (also known as the cotton mouth); the coral snakes; and the

Place the tablet back as far in the mouth as possible. Gently hold mouth shut until the tablet is swallowed.

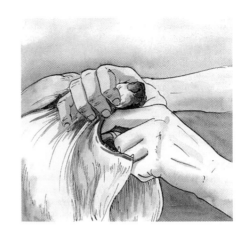

colubrids. The pit vipers and coral snakes are the most important. Rattlesnake bites occur most frequently in dogs in the west and southwest, where rattlesnakes are common. The snake's bite produces painful, slit-like puncture wounds that rapidly become swollen. Common symptoms of snakebite include immediate severe pain, swelling, darkened tissue coloration, and tissue necrosis (tissue death).

Urgent, immediate veterinary attention is necessary. The lethality of the snakebite depends on the type of venom, its toxicity, the amount of venom injected, the size and health of the animal bitten, and how much time passes from when the animal is bitten until it receives veterinary care. Poisonous snakebites require antivenin and antibiotic treatments. If the bite is left untreated, the skin and underlying tissue may turn dark and slough off (rot). However, the amount of venom injected (envenomization) cannot be determined simply by the appearance of the bite wound. The bite victim may become weak and exhibit various neurological signs, such as respiratory depression, and eventually go into shock and die.

If a venomous snake bites Lily, contact your veterinarian immediately. Most veterinarians who practice in areas where snakebites are common keep antivenin available. All dogs bitten by venomous snakes should be hospitalized and monitored for at least 24 hours.

Toad poisoning. Poisonous toads in the United States include the Colorado Rim Toad and the Marine Toad. The most toxic toad varieties are located in the southwestern desert, the southeastern United States, and Hawaii. If you suspect Lily has come in contact with a poisonous toad, contact a veterinarian immediately for specific treatment recommendations.

Lizard bites. The poisonous Gila Monster lizard is found in the southwestern United States. It has grooved teeth (instead of fangs) with which it holds onto its victims. Most dogs are bitten on the upper lip. The Gila Monster bite is extremely painful. No antivenin is available. Contact your veterinarian immediately for supportive treatment, antibiotics, and treatment to prevent shock.

Spiders. The brown spiders (Fiddleback, Brown Recluse, and Arizona Brown Spider) all are found in the southern United States. There is no antidote available for their venomous bites. Black Widow spiders are found throughout the United States. There is an antivenin available for Black Widow bites.

If Lily is bitten by one of these spiders, take her to a veterinarian immediately for emergency care, antibiotic therapy, and antivenin therapy (for Black Widow spider bite).

The Senior Lhasa Apso

With tender loving care, good nutrition, and a little luck, your Lhasa Apso may live for 12 to 16 years or more. Just like people, some dogs age more slowly than others, especially those that have received good health care throughout their lives. As a general rule, a Lhasa Apso is not quite a senior citizen until it reaches seven years of age. At this time, you may begin to notice changes beginning to take place in your pet's behavior, activity level, and physical stature. She may become arthritic, begin to slow down, and sleep more. She may develop problems with urination or bowel movements. Teeth and gums will require more attention due to accumulation of plaque and tartar on the teeth. The hair coat may become thinner, the skin less supple, and warts and other skin growths may appear. Cataracts become visible, hearing may diminish, and your friend will rely more on her sense of smell. These are all signs of the aging process.

As Lily's body ages, it undergoes a slowing of metabolic rate that can lead to weight gain; a weaker heart and a reduction in kidney and liver function; general muscle weakening and atrophy; and a gradual deterioration in condition with a decreased resistance to diseases. Lily may even show signs of disorientation or senility. All of these age-related changes, and the rate at which they occur, vary between individuals and are influenced by genetics, nutrition, environment, and the type of health care received in earlier years.

Golden Years Care

There are a number of things you can do to keep Lily comfortable in her golden years.

1. Provide a soft, warm bed. Cold temperatures and hard surfaces make arthritis more painful.

2. Weigh Lily monthly and do not allow her to become over- or underweight.

3. Take Lily out regularly for easy, short walks on level, soft, nonslippery surfaces (such as grass). Keep her toenails trimmed.

4. Do not make Lily jump up on furniture, climb stairs, or walk on slippery surfaces.

5. Feed Lily a diet appropriate for her age and health condition. Old dogs have an increase in protein requirement. An increase in protein quality and quantity recently has been demonstrated to be beneficial for some geriatric dogs, as well as having anticancer and antidiabetes effects.

6. Schedule physical examinations for Lily every six months in her geriatric years. This will enable you to detect and address any age-related problems (such as cataracts and heart or kidney insufficiency) early. Remember that

Older animals often develop arthritis. They need soft warm beds and sometimes special pain relievers.

Your Lhasa Apso will leave an indelible mark in your heart.

older dogs are more sensitive to anesthesia, especially if they are overweight.

7. If Lily has failing eyesight or is hard of hearing, make every effort not to startle her. Speak to her reassuringly as you approach so she knows you are there.

Euthanasia—When It's Time to Say Good-bye

Euthanasia means putting an animal to death humanely, peacefully, and painlessly. Euthanasia is usually done by first giving the animal a sedative to make it sleep deeply and then giving it a lethal substance by injection that ends its life almost instantly.

Even with the best care in the world, the sad day will come when you must consider euthanasia for your beloved companion. Understandably, this will be an emotionally painful time for you, because you will feel helpless in your inability to help your friend anymore, you will not want her to suffer for a moment, yet you cannot bear the thought of life without her. Nevertheless, if you begin to ask yourself whether your pet should be euthanized, there must be good reasons. The decision of when to euthanize is a difficult one that depends on many things. A good rule of thumb is, if suffering cannot be relieved, or if the quality of life is poor, or if the "bad days" simply outnumber the "good days," it is time to discuss euthanasia with your veterinarian. Your veterinarian can answer any specific questions you or your family may have. Your veterinarian can also help you if you wish to find a pet cemetery or desire cremation services.

During this emotional time, remember to take care of yourself and allow time to grieve. If you have children in the family, deal with the issue of animal loss at a level they can understand, comfort them, and let them share their grief. Take comfort in the knowledge that you took excellent care of your Lhasa Apso.

Selected Diseases and Conditions in Lhasa Apsos

Lhasa Apsos are strong, sturdy, resilient dogs. But like every other breed of dog, or animal species, Lhasa Apsos can have problems. Each breed of dog is predisposed to various conditions or disorders. This simply means that when there are problems, these are the types most commonly observed in the breed. So don't let these potential problems frighten you. Most likely, Lily will not have any of these conditions, but if she does, your ability to recognize these problems at the onset will enable your veterinarian to begin an appropriate course of treatment immediately.

To be an acceptable member of society, Lotus should learn some basic manners. Because Lhasa Apsos are extremely bright and eager to please, basic training is easy. But don't forget that Lhasa Apsos are easily excited, so don't let Lotus get distracted. He will astound you with how quickly he learns his lessons, as long as he stays focused. The best way to keep Lotus's attention is to keep training sessions short, make them fun and interesting, and always end on a positive note.

When teaching your Lhasa to heel, use quick, deliberate motions and an authoritative voice. Position your Lhasa on your left side, maintaining a short leash for instant corrective action.

Training a Lhasa Apso begins the moment you bring one home. It is never too early to start with simple, basic lessons. Studies have shown, for example, that leash training is easiest when a puppy is anywhere from five to nine weeks of age.

A basic puppy class, or dog training class, is the most effective way to begin obedience training and to teach Lotus to pay attention. There are as many different training techniques as there are dogs and trainers.

Dog training classes are a lot of fun. They are rewarding not only because your canine becomes a model citizen, but also because you will form many long-lasting friendships. Here are some training guidelines to get you started.

Come

Lotus must first learn his name so he can come when he is called and later respond to your commands. Start by calling his name when you feed him. It won't take him long to associate his name with a pleasant experience. In the beginning, you may also use small tidbits as a reward, along with much praise, when Lotus comes to you. Don't

show him that you have a food reward. Keep him guessing. Over time, decrease the frequency of food rewards, but continue the praise. In no time at all, Lotus will come to you when called, purely for the attention you bestow on him, but that doesn't mean you still can't occasionally surprise him with a very small food reward!

Sit

The *sit* command is the easiest of all commands to teach your Lhasa. With some patience and consistency, Lotus will probably grasp the general idea and learn to sit (if even for a brief time) in one to three training sessions.

Start by holding a small piece of food over his nose and raising your hand over his head. As his head goes up to follow the tidbit, his hindquarters will naturally go down and you may apply gentle pressure on the rump to help him sit in the beginning. Give Lotus a tidbit reward as soon as he is seated.

The trick here is to keep Lotus from jumping up in his excitement to grab the treat from you. You may need to start over a few times, applying slight pressure on his rump to keep him in place and remind him that he must remain in a sitting position for more than a few seconds!

Down

Teach Lotus to lie down by starting him in a sitting position. Kneel down alongside of him, on his right-hand side, facing the same direction, and rest your hand lightly on his shoulders. If it is more comfortable for you to stand, and if Lotus is accustomed to a grooming table, you can teach him the *down* command on the table, so you won't have to kneel down on the ground. Show Lotus a food reward and then slowly lower the food to the ground (or table surface) on which he is standing. This should encourage him to lie down to reach the food, but in the beginning you may have to apply light pressure to the top of his shoulders or pull one foreleg gently out in front of him. Once Lotus is in the *down* position, praise him and give him a food reward. As with other commands, you will eventually replace the food reward with praise alone.

Stay

Once Lotus has learned the *sit* and *down* commands very well, you can begin teaching him to *stay*. At first he will be confused because for most of his early training you have been asking him to come to you. Now you are going to ask him to remain where he is. To avoid injury, do not teach Lotus this command on the tabletop. He will not always obey your *stay* command and might jump off the table and be injured.

Make Lotus lie down on the floor and while placing your hand firmly on top of his shoulders, tell him to "*Stay.*" For the first few training sessions, if Lotus remains in place with

Repetition and praise for performing well is the best way to teach your dog to stay. As you practice, gradually increase the distance and length of time you maintain the command.

your hand on his shoulders for a full minute, then he deserves lots of praise.

For the next few lessons, make Lotus lie down and tell him to stay, then back away from him about 3 feet (1 meter) and wait one minute. If he jumps up to run to you, gently return him to his assigned place and tell him to stay, while simultaneously keeping your hand on his shoulder.

After Lotus has learned to stay in place for one minute with you seated a few feet in front of him, begin to lengthen the time period as well as your distance from him. If he starts to leave his designated spot, tell him to stay and raise your hand so that the palm of your hand is facing him. It won't take him long to associate the word with the hand signal and make the association that he is to remain in place until you call him and praise him for his good behavior.

THE TALENTED LHASA APSO

Lhasa Apsos are not only wonderful watchdogs and charming companions, they are attractive, clever, and dynamic. There is no limit to the things they can learn to do, and they excel at showing off their good looks. So let's take a look at some of the fun ways you can put Lotus's talents to the test!

Dog Shows

Dog shows are a lot of fun for both exhibitors and observers. Dogs are judged on how closely they come to the ideal standard for conformation for their breeds. If Lotus is handsome enough to compete against the best of his breed, consider joining a Lhasa Apso club, as well as a local kennel club. These clubs can provide you with information on show dates and locations, judges, professional handlers, canine activities, and even offer handling classes to teach you and your dog the ropes. Dog clubs also organize fun matches—dog shows where you can practice and perfect what you've learned before you participate in

Lhasa Apsos are intelligent and dynamic. They are limited only by the skills of their trainers!

an all-breed or specialty (one breed only, in your case, Lhasa Apsos) show.

Fun Matches

You can prepare yourself and your puppy for a future in the conformation ring by attending fun matches. Fun matches are just that—fun! They are hosted by American Kennel Club (AKC) approved breed clubs and are conducted according to American Kennel Club show rules. Only purebred, AKC registered dogs may participate. However, fun matches do not count toward points for a championship and dogs that have won points toward a championship do not compete. Judges at fun matches may be official AKC judges, or knowledgeable dog breeders, or handlers selected by the hosting club. Fun matches are a great way for you and your puppy to practice all aspects of a real dog show, from traveling to grooming, to exhibiting to winning!

Specialty Shows

Under the American Kennel Club show regulations, there are two types of conformation shows, which include specialty and group shows, and all-breed shows. Dogs are judged according to their breed standard and, by a process of elimination, one dog is selected as Best of Breed.

A specialty show is limited to a designated breed or grouping of breeds. For example, the Lhasa Apso Club of America holds an annual show for Lhasa Apsos only. The show is held under AKC rules and held by the individual breed clubs.

The Lhasa Apso Club of America is responsible for maintaining the official standards of the breed. If there are any changes or revisions to be made, the club must approve them before submitting them for final approval to the AKC.

To become a champion, a Lhasa Apso must win a minimum of 15 points by competing in formal American Kennel Club sanctioned, licensed events. The points must be accumulated as major wins under different judges.

All-Breed Shows

As the name implies, all-breed shows are for all breeds. Judging is conducted according to AKC rules. In addition to Best of Breed winners, open shows offer the titles of Best in Group (for dogs considered to be the best representative of their group) and Best in Show (for the dog selected as the best representative of its breed and group, compared to all other dogs of other breeds and groups).

Most dogs competing in Specialty or Open shows are competing for points toward their championship. A dog can earn from one to five points at a show. The number of points available depends upon the number of entries. Wins of three, four, or five points are called "majors." The fifteen points required for a championship title must be won under at least three different judges and include two majors won under two different judges.

There are five different classes in which a dog can compete for championship points and the classes are divided by sex:

✔ Puppy class (divided into 6–9 months of age and 9–12 months of age)
✔ Novice
✔ Bred by exhibitor
✔ American bred
✔ Open

Male dogs are judged first in this order: Puppy dogs, Novice dogs, Bred by exhibitor dogs, American bred dogs, and Open dogs. The first place winners in each class return to the showring to compete against each other in what is called the Winners Class. The dog selected as the best male in the Winners Class is the Winners Dog. This is the dog that will win the championship points in the show. The male that placed second to the Winners Dog in his original class (that is, Puppy, Novice, Bred by exhibitor, American bred, or Open) is then brought in to join the Winners Class and compete against the remaining four dogs in the class. The dog that wins second place in the Winners Class is the Reserve Winners Dog. If, for any reason, the AKC disallows the championship points to the Winners Dog, the Reserve Winners Dog will receive the points. The same procedure is then followed, in the same order, for the females, and the Winners Bitch (who also wins championship points) and Reserve Winners Bitch are selected.

The Winners Dog and Winners Bitch then join a class called the Best of Breed. In this class are entered dogs and bitches that already have won their championship titles. The judge selects either the Winners Dog or the Winners Bitch to be Best of Winners and finishes the judging by selecting from the group an animal to be Best of Breed. If the Best of Breed winner is a male, the judge selects the best bitch to be Best of Opposite Sex to the Best of Winners. If the Best of Breed winner is a female, the judge selects a male for Best of Opposite Sex to the Best of Winners.

At an all-breed show, judging takes place for each breed, then each Best of Breed winner competes in its breed group. The seven breed groups are:

✔ Sporting group
✔ Hound group
✔ Working group
✔ Terrier group
✔ Toy group
✔ Non-sporting group
✔ Herding group

The first place winners of each breed group then compete against each other for the coveted title of "Best in Show."

Obedience Trials

In these competitions, it's intelligence that counts. Dogs are put through a series of exercises and commands and judged according to how well they perform. Each dog starts out with 200 points. Points are deducted throughout the trials for lack of attention, nonperformance, barking, or slowness.

Obedience trials are divided into three levels increasing in difficulty: Novice—Companion Dog (C.D.), Open—Companion Dog Excellent (C.D.X.), and Utility—Utility Dog (U.D.).

To earn a C.D. title, the dog must be able to perform six exercises: heel on leash, stand for examination, heel free, recall, long sit, and long down. To earn a C.D.X. title the dog must be able to heel free, drop on recall, retrieve on flat, retrieve over the high jump, broad jump, long sit, and long down. To earn a U.D., the dog must be able to respond to signal exercise, scent discrimination tests, directed retrieve, directed jumping, and group examination. The dog must earn three legs to receive its title. To receive a leg the dog must earn at least 170 points out of a possible perfect score of 200, and receive more than 50 percent on each exercise.

Agility Competitions

Agility competitions are lots of fun and extremely popular. They are exciting, fast-paced, challenging, timed events. Dogs complete obstacle courses, jump over objects, teeter on seesaws, cross bridges, run through tunnels, and weave through poles. Titles that can be earned, in increasing level of difficulty, are: Novice Agility (NA), Open Agility (OA), Agility Excellent (AX), and Master Agility Excellent (MX).

Games

Lhasa Apsos enjoy all kinds of games, from hide-and-seek to fetch. Sprite, lively, dynamic, and full of fun, your Lhasa Apso will surprise and delight you with his ingenuity and creativity, earning his place in your heart as your favorite playmate.

Kennel and Breed Clubs

American Lhasa Apso Club
Membership
Joyce Johanson
126 Kurlene Drive
Macomb, IL 61455
(309) 837-1665
www.lhasaapso.org

American Lhasa Apso Club
Rescue
Mary Schroeder
5395 S. Miller Street
Littleton, CO 80127

American Kennel Club (AKC)
Registrations
5580 Centerview Drive
Raleigh, NC 27606-3390
(919) 233-9767
www.akc.org

The Canadian Kennel Club
89 Skyway Avenue, Suite 100
Etobicoke, Ontario, Canada
M9W6R4
(416) 675-5511

Federation Cynologique Internationale
Secretariat General de la FCA
Place Albert 1er, 13
B-6530 Thuin, Belgium
www.fci.be/english

The Kennel Club
1-4 Clargis Street, Picadilly
London W7Y 8AB England

States Kennel Club
1007 W. Pine Street
Hattiesburg, MS 39401
(601) 583-8345

United Kennel Club (UKC)
100 East Kilgore Road
Kalamazoo, MI 49001-5598
(616) 343-9020

United States Dog Agility Association
P.O. Box 850955
Richardson, TX 75085-8955
(972) 231-9700
Fax: (214) 503-0161
E-mail: *info@usdaa.com*
www.usdaa.com

Health Related Associations and Foundations

American Society for the Prevention of Cruelty
    to Animals (ASPCA)
424 East 92nd Street
New York, NY 10128-6804
(212) 876-7700
www.aspca.org

American Veterinary Medical Association
    (AVMA)
930 North Meacham Road
Schaumberg, IL 60173
www.avma.org

Canine Eye Registration Foundation (CERF)
South Campus Court, Building C
West Lafayette, IN 47907

National Animal Poison Control Center (NAPCC)
Animal Product Safety Service
1717 South Philo Road, Suite 36
Urbana, IL 61802
(888) 4ANI-HELP
(888) 426-4435
(900) 680-0000
(Consultation fees apply, call for details)
www.napcc.aspca.org

Orthopedic Foundation for Animals (OFA)
2300 Nifong Boulevard
Columbia, MO 65201
www.prodogs.com

Lost Pet Registries

The American Kennel Club (AKC)
AKC Companion Recovery
5580 Centerview Drive, Suite 250
Raleigh, NC 27606-3394
(800) 252-7894
E-mail: *found@akc.org*
www.akc.org/car.htm

Home Again Microchip Service
(800) LONELY-ONE

National Dog Registry (NDR)
P.O. Box 118
Woodstock, NY 12498-0116
(800) 637-3647

Petfinders
368 High Street
Athol, NY 12810
(800) 223-4747

Periodicals

The Lhasa Bulletin
The American Lhasa Apso Club
E-mail: *goldentu@lakefield.new*

The American Kennel Club Gazette
51 Madison Avenue
New York, NY 10010

Dog Fancy
Subscription Division
P.O. Box 53264
Boulder, CO 80323-3264
(303) 786-7306/666-8504
www.dogfancy.com

Dogs USA Annual
P.O. Box 55811
Boulder, CO 80322-5811
(303) 786-7652

Dog World
29 North Wacker Drive
Chicago, IL 60606
(312) 726-2802

Books

The Complete Dog Book. Official Publication of the American Kennel Club. New York, NY: Howell Book House, 1992.

Helf, Sally Ann. *Lhasa Lore*. Loveland, CO: Alpine Publications, 1983.

Herbel, Norman and Carolyn. *The New Complete Lhasa Apso*. New York, NY: Howell Book House, 1993.

Sefton, Frances. *The Lhasa Apso*. Australia: MacArthur Press, 1975.

I N D E X

Important Note

This book is concerned with selecting, keeping, and raising Lhasa Apsos. The publisher and the authors think it is important to point out that the advice and information for Lhasa Apso maintenance applies to healthy, normally developed animals. Anyone who acquires an adult dog or one from an animal shelter must consider that the animal may have behavioral problems and may, for example, bite without any visible provocation. Such anxiety-biters are dangerous for the owner as well as the general public.

Caution is further advised in the association of children with dogs, in meetings with other dogs, and in exercising the dog without a leash.

About the Authors

Stephen Wehrmann is a veterinarian practicing in St. Petersburg, Florida. After graduating from the University of Hawaii with a B.A. in zoology, he received his doctorate of veterinary medicine from the University of Missouri. A frequent lecturer to pet groups, Dr. Wehrmann has also authored many articles regarding companion animal care that have appeared in regional and national publications.

Sharon Vanderlip, D.V.M., has provided veterinary care to domestic and exotic animal species for more than 20 years. She has written books and published articles in scientific and lay publications. Dr. Vanderlip served as the Associate Director of Veterinary Services for the University of California at San Diego School of Medicine; has worked on collaborative projects with the Zoological Society of San Diego; has owned a private veterinary practice; is former Chief of Veterinary Services for the National Aeronautics and Space Administration (NASA), and is a consultant in reproductive medicine and surgery for various research and wildlife projects, including the Endangered Red Wolf project. Dr. Vanderlip has lectured at kennel clubs and veterinary associations throughout the United States and Europe on topics in canine medicine and is the recipient of various awards for her writing and dedication to animal health.

Photo Credits

Pets By Paulette: pages 2–3, 5, 12 bottom left, 12 top, 13 top, 17, 25, 32 top left, 36, 37 top right, 40 top, 41 top right, 44 top, 45, 48 bottom left, 49 top left, 53, 56 top left, 57, 61 top, 61 bottom left, 61 bottom right, 65, 72 top left, 72 bottom left, 72 bottom right, 73 bottom left, 88, 89; Tara Darling: pages 4, 8, 9, 20 bottom left, 32 bottom left, 37 bottom right, 41 bottom right, 44 bottom left, 49 bottom, 52, 60 top left, 60 bottom left, 64, 68, 73 top, 76, 77, 84, 85; Norvia Behling: pages 16, 21 bottom right, 24, 48 bottom right; Kent and Donna Dannen: pages 13 bottom right, 20 top left, 21 top right, 28, 29, 33 top left, 33 bottom left, 33 bottom right, 40 bottom right, 48 top, 49 top right, 56 bottom left, 60 top right, 60 bottom right, 72 top right, 73 bottom right.

Cover Credits

Front cover: Tara Darling; Inside front cover: Tara Darling; Inside back cover: Kent and Donna Dannen; Back cover: Pets By Paulette.

Acknowledgments

I would like to thank my husband, Jack Vanderlip, D.V.M., for his invaluable help as an expert consultant, and my editor, Mark Miele. As always, their ideas and suggestions contributed significantly to the quality of the manuscript and are greatly appreciated.

All inquiries should be addressed to:
Barron's Educational Series, Inc.
250 Wireless Boulevard
Hauppauge, NY 11788
http://www.barronseduc.com

International Standard Book No. 0-7641-1958-3

Library of Congress Catalog Card No. 2001043511

Library of Congress Cataloging-in-Publication Data
Wehrmann, Stephen.
   Lhasa Apsos : a complete pet owner's manual: everything about purchase, care, nutrition, behavior, and training / Stephen Wehrmann ; illustrations by Michele Earle-Bridges. — 2nd ed. / revised by Sharon L. Vanderlip.
      p. cm.
Includes bibliographical references (p.).
ISBN 0-7641-1958-3 (alk. paper)
   1. Lhasa apso. I. Vanderlip, Sharon Lynn. II. Title.
SF429.L5 W44   2002
636.72—dc21   2001043511

Printed in China
9 8 7 6